KITING THE HURRICANE

DOM MEE

Copyright © Dom Mee 2015

All rights reserved. This book, or any portion thereof, may not be reproduced or used in any manner whatsoever without the express written permission of the publisher, except for the use of brief quotations in a book review.

Book layout by www.ebooklaunch.com

First Printing, 2015

ISBN 10 1519394365
ISBN 13 9781519394361

Kew Villas Publishing
Kew Villas & Estates Ltd
36 Lighthouse Street
Galle Fort
Galle
Sri Lanka

www.dommee.co.uk

Table of Contents

Acknowledgments i
Foreword iii
The Messenger 1
Chasing Arctic Ghosts 4
Return to Suez 13
As High as a Kite 16
Big Roll of the Dice 21
It's Not the Size of the Dog 24
Kiting the Grand Beast 29
First Punch 33
Hurricane Ally 38
Russian Roulette 43
Into the Abyss 48
The Demon 52
Death Sentence 58
Dark Spiral 64
The Button 68
The Miracle 76
Angels and the Unpaid Ferryman 82
Back on the Foredeck 88
Return of the Prodigal Daughter 91
Restoration 96
Epilogue 101

Acknowledgments

It is difficult not to forget the many people who helped me along the way with Kite Quest 200. From the bottom of my heart, if you are not mentioned, please forgive me, but my memory is rather rubbish and is getting worse as the years roll by.

To the team that came together to make this even possible—my wife at the time, Ang, and Titch Wibrew being behind the project from day one—I couldn't have done it without you. I also thank the following people:

The build team at Justin Adkin's yard in Exmouth: lead builder Jamie Frabrizio, supported by Emily Adkin, for making the world's toughest boat.

Phil Morrison for designing a boat with incredible performance and the ability to sail in major offshore conditions.

Mike Broughton for all the weather support and for being the friend on the other end of the satellite phone during my lowest times.

Louay Habib for just being Louay.

The team at Joint Rescue Coordination Centre Halifax, Nova Scotia for organising my rescue: Captain Athaide Ainsley and the crew of the *Berg Nord* for being the first to respond to my distress.

Rescue Flights 313 and 116, my guardians in the sky.

Captain Brian Penney and the crew of Canadian Coast Guard Ship *Cygnus* for retrieving me from hell and for your kindness on board your fine ship.

The Falmouth Coast Guard in England for registering my EPIRB and coordinating with JRCC.

To all my sponsors and friends: John Wrelton at Wilkie May & Tuckwood, Peter Beardow of 7E Communications, Stratos Global, BMW Westerly Exeter, GUL, Mike McDonald at Eimskip, Purple Marine, Panasonic Toughbook, Kiteship, Mel and Jim Murell of Intotec, Peter Lynn kites, Rick Lecoat at Shark Attack design, Esporta, Bang the Corner, Winning Wind, Neil Grant at Hunter Air Canada Cargo, Alby McCracken of Para Anchors Australia, Misha Mouratov and Olga White, Cruga Biltong, Garmin, Veneziani, Leeside Manor

Hotel, Empire Signs, Barry Roche of Interclean, Sea Vision UK, British Waterbed Company, Frank Hatcher of Avolon, Sharky Ward at Inform, Barton Marine, Dave Hay at the Royal Marines Boat House, Uri Geller, Her Majesty Queen Elizabeth II for wishing me luck, and the bar flies of the White Horse pub in Bradford on Tone.

To all the people who took the time to send words of encouragement while I was on the voyage, it really helped to keep me going.

The writing of this book has been a journey that nearly didn't happen. Thanks to Donna Beech for pushing me to write for 10 years; you finally got through.

I would also like to thank all my friends who helped contribute to this book, as well as fellow Royal Marine writer "Mark Time" for helping me stitch my story together and mentoring me through the writing process. It has been a very emotional journey recounting events, but at the same time, it has been an incredibly liberating experience. I would encourage everyone to write their story.

To my mum, dad, and my sister, Sian, thank you for always supporting me and never holding me back.

To my wife, Anna, and my sons, Dimitri, George, and Laurence, you have helped my spirit to soar to a higher place than I could ever have imagined in my wildest dreams. I am truly blessed.

Foreword

I've been asked many times by friends why I've never written a book on my adventures. The short answer is that I've never had the time. My life since leaving the Royal Marines has been fluid like a river advancing forward. Like a shark, I've had to keep moving to stay alive.

It's hard for me to believe that 10 years have passed since I was on my ill-fated voyage across the North Atlantic. It was a very powerful experience and an incredibly harrowing time. When I started doing major expeditions, I was very interested in the inner journey and always curious about whether, after a long voyage, I'd recognise myself at the other end. I would refer to this time in my life as the "wilderness years." The Australian Aboriginals call it a "walkabout," Native American Indians call it a "vision quest," and girls from Chelsea call it a "gap year." For me, it wasn't a rite of passage; I'd already entered into manhood as a Royal Marines Commando, but I'd always been part of a unit, a collective, an elite strike force. I'd been a part of this group since the age of 17, and I'd wanted to do something alone to truly find myself. This voyage of discovery was to take me to places I'd never heard of, enable me to make new friends in faraway lands, and offer me a unique insight into the world in which we live.

The journey was, however, incredibly dangerous. I was not, as accused by some people, an adrenaline junkie—far from it. I hated the dangerous parts of the path I chose. Who would want to be eaten alive by wild creatures or swept away by the mighty ocean?

I recall exchanging emails and ideas with Andrew McAuley, a fellow adventurer on his own voyage of discovery, who was kayaking from Australia to New Zealand. He'd left Australia crying like a child not because he was weak but because he'd understood the enormity of the task. He'd also known that it could be a one-way trip. It's at this stage that most people turn around—realising that it was too difficult to attempt. Not Andrew; he was pushing the boundaries on every level. As a hard-core kayaker, he wouldn't even have a cabin, and he would make history if he completed the challenge.

Andrew was sadly lost at sea just 37 miles from reaching New Zealand. He'd managed to kayak 963 miles, a feat that was described by some in the Coast Guard as "humanly impossible." Anyone who knows anything about the ocean would say that this was an amazing achievement. I cannot imagine what hardships he would have endured during this voyage. I was, however, stunned to see some of the hateful comments posted after Andrew was lost.

One cowardly anonymous rant left on a website finished with "And for those who say he died doing [what] he loved I doubt that was what he was thinking as his lungs filled with water. He was no doubt thinking about his wife, son and friends, therefore the moments before he died were the only moments of sanity in his pathetic life. There was only one thing worthy for this man and he got it."

He didn't know Andrew, so why would he be so hateful towards him and hurtful towards Andrew's grieving wife? Apart from his clear lack of humanity, the simple answer is this: the herd fears people who are different. If people don't play by the rules, they are a threat. But some people don't want to be in the herd; some people like to live on the fringe. And you don't kayak a thousand miles across one of the roughest stretches of water in the world unless you are very much on top of your game. Andrew's son can be justifiably proud of his father

I ended up on the fringe by default because of the path I took. It was a place of extremes and incredible people—people unknown to the majority. There were men and women out there rowing the North Pacific, kayaking the North Atlantic, walking to the North Pole, climbing K2 without oxygen, swimming the Amazon, being the first to sail solo around the world, and surfing the biggest waves. I enjoyed their company. Everyone had a different story about how they ended up on this side of the human condition. Many question why people do extreme adventures and often mock those who strive to push the boundaries of human capabilities. There is no easy answer. Maybe it is something in our DNA that pushes some of us to go off and make the impossible possible. This risk taking has driven humans to the top of the food chain. We all take risks every day, but as part of our daily routines, we rarely acknowledge them. Amongst the many quotes, American novelist Judith McNaught touches on the point: "You can't outwit fate by standing on the sidelines placing little side bets about the outcome of life. Either you wade in and risk everything you have to play the game or you don't play at all. And if you don't play you can't win." I wasn't able to find any inspirational quotes about not taking risks.

For me, the call of the ocean became so loud that I could not shut it out. It was my church, my sanity; it was somewhere I actually fitted in. The deep and mysterious ocean does not tolerate egos; it strips you bare. It's a violent father and a loving mother, but it's always hungry for the souls of men.

The 2005 hurricane season claimed around 4,000 lives and changed thousands of others in the wake of its fury. The communities of the southern United States of America are still rebuilding and coming to terms with what happened that year.

I was spared. This is my story...

For Andrew

"For most seagulls, life consists simply of eating and surviving. Flying is just a means of finding food.
However, Jonathan Livingston Seagull is no ordinary bird.
For him, flying is life itself.
Against the conventions of seagull society, he seeks to find a higher purpose and become the best at doing what he loves."

- Richard Bach

For Kieron Blight:

"I see you every day. In a child's smile. In a good deed.
In an act of compassion. In all things decent in this world,
I see you, and in the light monsoon breeze,
I feel you."

- Dom Mee

The Messenger

July 2005

The hurricane season has started two months early this year. Tropical storms have already smashed into Mexico and Florida. Tropical Storm Arlene brushes over Cuba and hits the Florida Panhandle like a probing attack for a much larger force. Tropical Storm Bret tests the coastal defences, landing in Veracruz, Eastern Mexico, killing two people, and flooding hundreds of homes. Tropical Storm Cindy is briefly promoted to hurricane status, making landfall in Louisiana, causing power blackouts, and killing three victims in its wake. The people of Louisiana probably think they have dodged a bullet as Cindy is only a category 1 hurricane. While these storms alone can be seen as catastrophic, this is only the beginning of the nightmare that will unfold...

With conditions worsening, the National Weather Center is observing a lot more activity, signalling potential severe weather forming in the Atlantic. Hurricane Dennis has already triggered deadly flooding in Haiti. Millions watch TV in horror as mudslides sweep down the mountains of Jamaica as the hurricane strengthens. Dennis is growing in intensity and is upgraded to a category 4 hurricane when it hits Cuba. Now a monster storm with powerful 140mph winds, it destroys everything in its path. Six hundred thousand Cubans flee to the high ground as Dennis churns its way across the island. The brunt of the hurricane misses the US Naval Station at Guantanamo Bay, where a detention facility houses suspected Al Qaeda terrorists and their sympathisers who were captured in Afghanistan. The storm careers across the mountains of Pinar del Rio and is finally downgraded to a category 1 hurricane.

Dennis leaves Cuba for open water, but its rampage across the island nation has devastated 120,000 homes. The cost of the damage stands at approximately $1.4 billion US dollars. Even worse, 16 lives have been lost. In a televised appearance, the Cuban leader, Fidel Castro, states that if Dennis had passed directly over the capital, this total would have increased to $3 billion. He reports that some 1,531,000 people have been evacuated throughout the country and a forced diaspora of 245,106 relocated to hostels and relatives' homes. Emergency aid is offered from around the world, but Castro, true to his spirit of independence, rejects all help from the West, only allowing assistance from his old friend and comrade, President Hugo Chavez of Venezuela.

Dennis is far from finished. It enters the Gulf of Mexico, increasing in size as it sucks up more moisture from the ocean. It sets its sights on the United States of America (US). The hurricane is expected to brush past the keys and slam the US coast along the Florida Panhandle, which was hammered by Hurricane Ivan the previous year.

"When Dennis gets into the Gulf of Mexico, this will be a whole statewide problem," says Florida State meteorologist Ken Nelson. "This is going to be a very large storm like Ivan."

Reports state that NASA is deciding on whether to delay the scheduled launch of the space shuttle *Discovery* at Cape Canaveral on Florida's Atlantic coast. It will be the first shuttle flight since the Columbia accident in 2003. If the launch is delayed, *Discovery* will be returned to its hangar for safety as Dennis passes through.

In Key West, the party is in full swing, with Duval Street packed with partygoers from all over the US. Cindy Fairbanks is working hard on Wednesday night, trying to keep everybody served with beer at the Bull and Whistle, while Elvis impersonator Bobby J entertains the large crowd.

"Cindy, have you seen the news? There's a hurricane heading to the keys," Yankee Jack shouts across the bar.

"No way. God damn it." Cindy is a hurricane veteran. Like others, she's been through all this before, and the people of the keys know what preparations to make.

The National Hurricane Warning Center forecasts a storm surge of four to seven metres, accompanied by isolated tornados just for good measure. The next day, emergency management officials order the evacuation of the keys. Evacuation orders are also issued across the coastal areas of Florida and the Gulf of Mexico.

It is 5 pm, Thursday, the 7th of July. Key West is a ghost town. The party is over, and the airport is closed. The oil companies have already scrambled helicopters to airlift 1,000 oil workers from their oil platforms in the Gulf of Mexico as Dennis roars its way across the ocean.

Dennis finally makes landfall at Santa Rosa Island; Okaloosa and Escambia are the first Florida counties to be hit by the hurricane's eye wall. Due to an unusually small eye, the region is thankfully spared more major destruction. The residents of Fort Walton Beach and Pensacola who remain in the region are told just hours before the storm's arrival that storm shelters are full, and they are urged to stay home or find other shelter. In Escambia County, the officials announce that they are no longer able to respond to 911 calls for help due to the high winds.

Dennis comes only 10 months after Hurricane Ivan struck the panhandle and Mobile Bay region. It hits just 50 miles east of Ivan's landfall, where recovery efforts from that storm are still ongoing. At landfall, Dennis matches Ivan's category 3 wind speeds. Power outages are reported in Mobile and across the panhandle. The Florida governor, Jeb Bush, promises in a televised press conference that all efforts will be made to restore power as quickly as possible. President Bush declares portions of Florida, Alabama, and Mississippi major disaster areas.

Hurricane Dennis finally runs out of steam. In its wake, the storm has killed 89 people from the US and the Caribbean and has caused over $4 billion in damage across the region. It is the biggest ever recorded hurricane in July.

Six days later, Hurricane Emily enters the Gulf of Mexico. It is even bigger than Dennis. This is no ordinary year. Hurricane Dennis is only a messenger for the worst hurricane season in history.

It will be a year in which all the records for the most powerful hurricanes will be smashed, and thousands of lives will be changed forever. The gods are angry, and they are going to vent their fury down on us mortals below.

Chasing Arctic Ghosts

August 2004, the High Arctic

I'd already unslung my .303 Lee Enfield rifle in readiness and stared across the bay. The winds had changed since we'd left on our overland trip to find the ship. The bay, fairly clear before, was now full of sea ice. We were completely cut off from our route back to the small Inuit settlement of Talyoak in the high Arctic.

This could be tricky, I thought. I told the expedition team we should set up camp for the night. I needed time to think.

It had been two months since we'd set out in search of an 1829 expedition led by Sir John Ross. He'd unfortunately taken a wrong turn in his search for the Northwest Passage and had become incarcerated in the ice with no way out. Ironically, we were trapped overlooking Victoria Harbour, where Ross came to grief and abandoned his ship, the *Victory*. With no other options available, Ross and the crew had to haul boats and equipment over 300 miles north out of the Arctic over sea ice, hoping to find a ship in the main channel of Lancaster Sound. One can only imagine the relief when the beleaguered party finally reached the open water to the north. One cannot imagine the devastation when they realised it was too late. All the ships in Lancaster Sound had left the area with the onset of winter.

Ross and his men, using what little equipment they had, constructed a small shelter in which to overwinter, and they named it Somerset House. The winter was harsh, even for the Arctic, with the outside temperature plummeting to -70. They battled hunger and boredom; however, a polar bear falling through the ceiling of their dwelling solved both.

The following spring, melting ice allowed them to head out into open water in the hope of finding a ship to rescue them. The *Isabella*, which was, by chance, the ship which was first commanded by Ross on his earlier expedition to find the passage, appeared on the horizon, and they were saved after spending three years in the Arctic.

It remains one of the greatest survival stories of Arctic exploration.

In comparison to Ross's nightmare, my expedition was a walk in the park. It would be easy for a layperson to think that technological advancement in clothing, equipment, and communications lessens the human instinct for survival in such an environment. It doesn't. We still had to be very astute; the Arctic is an unforgiving place. I had to consider our next move extremely carefully. We couldn't afford any injuries, and everybody had to be on high alert— we were deep in polar bear country. I was pondering our next move when Mark "Killer" Cowell, a good friend from the Royal Marines, said, "Why don't we just try to ram through in the boats?"

Why not? I thought. Trying to walk out with such heavy equipment would put unnecessary strain on the expedition.

We started off into the floes, and it seemed Killer's idea was working well. Although we were covering only one mile per hour, at least we were moving. I was planning another voyage through the Northwest Passage in a few years' time, and this was the perfect opportunity to look for ideas to help get through the ice floes. As we slowly battled through, I started to think that kites would work pretty well in such a situation. I'd read about kites being used by polar adventurers to aid their progress to the South Pole. Alan Chambers, a good friend from the Royal Marines who'd led many expeditions to the North Pole, had explained that kites weren't suitable for the northern Arctic because the pressure ridges in the sea ice made it impossible to use them. The difference between my maritime adventures and Alan's was that I needed open water, and he needed solid ground. In my world, kites *could* work in the sea ice—in theory.

Mark Hanky was sitting next to me as a living legacy of the original 1829 expedition. I first met Mark at the Royal Navy stand at the London Boat Show advertising the previous year's expedition in an effort to raise more funds for this trip. Mark just walked up to our stand, pointed at James Clarke Ross, and said simply, "That's my great-great grandfather."

I met him for a beer, and at the end of the night, I asked him if he wanted to come on the expedition and touch the legacy of his ancestors. He said yes on the spot.

Mark looked at me. "What are you thinking about?" He knew me well.

"Just some random ideas." I smiled.

Baz Campbell, my second in command on the expedition, knocked me back to reality. "Dom, check out Cronks."

Travelling through Thom Bay, which is renowned for having a large population of polar bears, I thought it prudent to position Paul "Cronks" Cronin on the shoreline armed with a Lee Enfield .303 rifle to scan and clear the way ahead. Cronks was on the high ground and was alerting us to the presence of a polar bear. We stopped immediately.

Weighing in at a metric tonne, polar bears are the largest recorded land carnivore on the planet. They can run at 30mph and complete most physical functions better than man. They are essentially unbeatable, and we took their presence very seriously on the expedition. A polar bear is one of the few animals on the planet that will hunt and kill humans. This was their world, and being rushed by a polar bear on the ice floes would probably cause a fatality among the team. Here, it was a clear and present danger.

To learn as much about the environment as possible, I'd spent a lot of time hunting with the Inuit before I'd started my 2003 solo kayak. The Inuit view bears as similar to humans—very smart but each individually unique.

Other than Inuit George Alukee, no hunters would move across Thom Bay due to the large bear population. An old Inuit born in Thom Bay, George and his family came every year to hunt. He wanted his sons and grandsons to learn the ways of Thom Bay, their historical land and spiritual home, even though they lived in the settlement of Talyoak. I'd become good friends with George and his wife, Elizabeth. They were both very warm and welcoming on both trips but had also offered stern warnings: "There are a lot of bears up there and some real mean ones. You'll have to kill the mean ones; they don't stop, and they keep coming back. They're very smart. If it comes back to your camp three times, you'll have to kill him or he'll kill you. Be careful, Umimmak."

Umimmak, which means "musk ox" in Inuktitut, became my Inuit name. I'd proved myself to be strong on land after I'd fought with one on my solo trip, and it had inadvertently become my rite of passage. I have to admit that I was very proud to have an Inuit name.

We pulled into the shore and joined Cronks and Craig Haslam. There, on the ice floes, was a large bear by a seal blowhole. The bear was around 8 to 10 feet and was probably a male, as most females would be with their cubs at this time of the year. A master of camouflage, he was covering his big black nose with his huge white paws while he lay there invisible. It's a marvel of nature.

The bear looked casually at the seven of us and went back to his seal watch, not in the least bit threatened by our presence. As he was blocking our route, we had to move him on. After firing a cracker shell to scare him, I chased after him, shouting and firing warning shots into the air. To watch this amazingly powerful creature jump gracefully in perpetual motion from floe to floe into the water, like a one-tonne ballerina, then up onto an iceberg was such a beautiful sight. Despite his retreat, polar bears aren't scared easily, and it was highly likely he would return if hungry.

We continued battling through the ice floes until Sue Cox, our historical researcher, fell through the ice. Baz saw her going over the side of the boat and quickly lunged across the MIB, managing to get a hand on her before hauling her back on board. The water temperature in the Arctic goes down to -2°C but doesn't freeze because of the salt content, so hypothermia would immediately have taken over upon her entry into the water. The currents in the bay could have easily sucked her under the floes, making it nigh on impossible to save her. It was a stark reminder of all the dangers out here.

With enough excitement for one day, it was time to strike camp and warm Sue up. The one advantage we had over the polar bears was that Baz, Cronks, Craig, and I were former Royal Marines, so securing a camp area was our forte. We prepared our camp as we would on an operational tour. Heading to the shore, we would drop off two men to undertake a clearance patrol to check not for enemy forces but for bears and to ascertain the suitability of the camp site. Once cleared, the signal would be given for the boats to approach and to then set up camp. To ward off inquisitive polar bears, we laid trip flares along the approaches to the camp. If anything tried to sneak in, the shotgun cartridges firing would certainly alert us. It was just as well; that evening, a mother and her cub nearly walked into the camp. Craig's warning shots encouraged them to move on.

Even after such an arduous day, such actions showed what a great team I had to work with, and their commitment was never in doubt. I finally settled down for the night, but it was difficult to sleep. The threat of polar bears wasn't even a consideration; I had kites on the brain. I was already looking at the next expedition.

"If you are going to walk on thin ice, you might as well dance."
- Inuit saying

***

Upon returning to the UK, I walked into the expedition office—a rather grand name for my garage. As usual, Titch Wibrew was busy trying to get more sponsorship.

"Welcome back, brother." I gave him a big hug—a most underrated greeting, often derided as being unmanly, yet one common to the many Alpha males I've had the privilege of knowing and people, like Titch, with whom I had a close connection. I live by the motto 'Real men hug.'

After the expedition debrief, I casually turned the conversation to something else. "Shipmate, can you get me as much information as you can muster on kites?"

"OK, boss." He rolled his eyes. Kites had never been mentioned before. I'd not been back 10 minutes, and he knew I was planning something new.

I'd first met Titch in 1992 when we'd served together in Belfast with 40 Commando during the "Troubles." His nickname, which was due to him being rather on the short side, originated all the way back to commando training. We'd followed each other around the corps, and after Belfast, we'd both been drafted to Poole, serving together for a year at Chivenor Barracks and working on the Provost staff, which allowed us both plenty of time to indulge our passion for surfing even when we were supposed to be working. On one occasion when "checking" the Saunton Sands rifle range, we'd sneaked off for a couple of hours in the surf. My duty phone rang as I was getting into my wetsuit. It was the RAF Police.

"We need to overnight a prisoner in your cells. We can be with you guys in less than an hour."

Overhearing the conversation, Titch was shaking his head vigorously.

"Sorry, mate," I said. "I'd love to help, but we've no cells available. You know what marines are like; the cells are full of reprobates." There was no way I was letting work interrupt surfing, even if I did have a guardroom of empty cells…

As I placed my phone back in my grab bag, I noted the kite surfers for the first time; they were jumping and skirting the waves, gaining terrific height off the surf. It looked fantastic. I made a mental note to check them out later.

Titch and I left the Royal Marines in 2002 within six months of each other. His small stature was no barrier to him becoming an accomplished cyclist representing the Royal Navy in mountain biking, but his main passion was skydiving. After a year working for a diving company, he was looking for another challenge and had managed to gain employment in the skydiving industry.

Preparation for my 2003 expedition to solo kayak deep into the Arctic made me realise that I needed help. And so it passed that Titch became my expedition project manager when he wasn't working at the drop zone. For the last 18 months, he'd been dealing with sponsors, the media, stores, and pretty much anything else.

My first initial research into kites showed that they could have a multitude of uses, but many were theoretical rather than proven practical applications. This excited me; well-travelled paths do not interest the adventurer inside. I trawled further. The downside of pioneering is that I spend lots of time banging my head against the wall, so I sought further advice from Peter Lynn in New Zealand, Flexi foil, and Kiteship.

The biggest headache seemed to be launching kites from a boat. It sounded so simple, yet it was the prominent problem I had to nail. These issues could have been one reason that so little of note had been achieved using kites—a fact also underlined during our research. No one had yet kited across an ocean; any attempt would be a world first. This alone could generate new sponsors and be the catalyst for even bigger expeditions.

Ideas were flowing. I had a Bosun dinghy, which had been kindly donated by Dave Hay at the Royal Marines Adventure Training Center. Dave taught me to sail in a Bosun dinghy after I'd returned from Iraq in 1991, and we'd remained friends borne by our love of the sea. Every spare bit of time I had was taken up with Dave at the boat shed. I was addicted to the water and loved the boat shed. Even when the weather was bad, I'd still go down for a cup of tea and to talk about sailing. Life was simple; they were happy times.

I decided that to save a little money, I could use the Bosun dinghy hull for my kite boat, but it needed to be built into a tank for an ocean crossing. I approached boat designer Phil Morrison to create a blueprint of a boat that could fly kites. Phil is a well-respected boat designer, part of the GBR Americas Cup team, and a sailor in his own right. I'd also rowed across the North Pacific with Tim Welford in a rowboat that Phil had designed.

Tim and I were in the same troop throughout commando training, and even though we never served together in the same unit, we'd kept in touch. He rowed the Atlantic with Wayne Callahan in 1997.

Sponsored by Ryvita, he named the boat *Crackers*. He then launched a campaign to row across the North Pacific—the K2 of ocean rowing. Unfortunately, his rowing partner dropped out, so he rang me to ask if I knew anybody who could step up. I was heavily involved in international yacht racing at the time, and having just finished a world championship series, I was at a loose end. Like an idiot, I said "What about me?"

We endured nearly five months at sea, encountering three typhoons. The boat stood up to the task, so I had full confidence that Phil was the man for the job.

In the meantime, I had fairly urgent matters to attend to, such as paying the mortgage. Returning from the Arctic, my wife at the time, Ang, gave me the grim news that our finances were pretty dire, as the expedition budget had overrun.

She'd held back telling me until I'd returned, as she knew that external pressures were the last thing an adventurer needed while away. "We need to take stock and go easy for a while," she said.

I agreed. Since leaving the Royal Marines, I'd set out to forge a new life as an adventurer. I'd generally scraped a living together through expedition sponsorship, yacht racing, and doing armed security for yachts that transited off the coast of Somalia—work that wasn't regular but paid well. In the first two years after leaving the Royal Marines, I was really struggling, as many ex-service personnel do in the new environment of "Civvy Street."

Things went from bad to worse until I reached out to a former Marine, Simon Jones, who'd established a really successful security company, IDS International Ltd. I approached him for sponsorship for my first solo expedition to the Arctic. In return, I would promote his company, generating as much publicity as possible. IDS International became our title sponsor, covering the wages for Titch and me while we organised the two Arctic expeditions in search of Ross. This had been a major lifeline for us; my life would have turned out very differently without his kindness. Happy with our media drive, he continued to sponsor us, allowing me to focus on future expeditions. Knowing that my mortgage was covered every month freed me up to get more sponsors to the table.

The early phases of the research and development for kiting were a total nightmare. It became clear why kiting hadn't yet become an adventurer's method of travel and why no one had ever crossed an ocean using one—it was a technically very difficult. The biggest problem was launching the kites on a boat while moving forward with the wind behind you. Normally, kite surfers swim away to create tension on the line and then launch their kites from the water. This was theoretically possible while moving forward on a boat, but the reality was far different and, at this stage, unachievable to the point where it seemed impossible.

To add to the growing list of problems, I had very little kiting experience. I had to start learning fast, which, while frustrating in the big scheme of preparing expeditions, was stacks of fun.

We had lots of trials with smaller kites to launch main kites. Peter Lynn in New Zealand was a great help; he introduced me to lots of different people in the kiting world and even sent me his own kite boat from New Zealand to assist with my trials. He was a great guy and was really passionate about kites.

In an effort to raise sponsorship, we displayed a small stand at the London Boat Show in Earls Court. It was always a great event where I would meet lots of people who were involved in similar adventures, and it was always fantastic fun reuniting with many of my old sailing buddies.

Titch and I set up the display, and this particular year, we were fortunate to be beside the Sunseeker stand. Sunseeker was always the star attraction of the show, and it was where they would show their multimillion-pound super yachts. These were clearly boats I'd never be able to afford in my life, and they drew in the crowds.

While our positioning was perfect, what was worrying was the fact that Simon hadn't paid our sponsorship cheque for three months. Titch and I had no money for the show, and we had past and potential sponsors to entertain. I'd already written a letter to the owner of Sunseeker, Robert Braithwaite, to see if he would help support our small stand. Robert was a true gentleman and, as someone who was really interested in what I did, agreed to assist.

The Sunseeker team was awesome. They allowed us to bring our sponsors to the Sunseeker executive lounge—*the* best place in the show—which also offered free drinks and food. This was absolutely fantastic, but we still had the problem of not being able to afford tickets for our potential sponsors to even get into the show.

By now, we were living by our wits—a term known in the Royal Marines as "cuffing it." We'd become friendly with the girls who ran the VIP entrance for Sunseeker. We'd discovered that if a potential Sunseeker buyer was turning up, they would be collected by a Bentley and taken to the Sunseeker private entrance and, as such, didn't need show tickets. Following the Royal Marines' mantra of "no cuff too tough," we approached the girls to pick up our sponsors in the Sunseeker Bentley to bring them to the VIP entrance, provided they were not busy with their own. Bingo! This not only saved us having to buy tickets but also impressed our sponsors, who felt like royalty.

As our main sponsor, we obviously gave Simon the red-carpet treatment. However, despite our champagne welcome, he arrived looking very stressed. I asked about the sponsorship money.

"Come to mine tonight where we can talk about it."

I knew something was seriously wrong. I spoke to Ang on the phone to say that I was meeting with Simon. She was very anxious and notified me that we'd reached our overdraft limit. So, it was understandable that I arrived at Simon's place a little worried.

Simon sat me down. He looked awful. "Mate, the business is going bust. I wish I could give you better news."

I was stunned, but I just reached out and gave him a hug. This was going to be a big fall for Simon, and I really felt for him. My mind in turmoil, I walked forlornly back to where Titch and I were staying. I rang Ang. She burst into tears on the phone.

It was horrible. *What the hell I am going to do now?*

Return to Suez

December, Alexandria, Egypt

My kiting project was looking like a mirage. Titch said he needed work, so he got some work as a skydiving instructor at the drop zone. I hit the phones to see if any work was kicking around. I applied for a job as a contractor in Iraq, as I was desperate to earn some money. I'd sent off my application and, with my experience, was sure I'd be offered a position pretty quickly. But it was something I really didn't want to do; there were many horror stories about contractors over there, but I blanked them out. I needed work before the bailiffs arrived.

By pure chance, on the way to a friend's wedding, I met a guy on the London underground with whom I'd done my parachute course 12 years before. We grabbed a quick coffee.

"What have you been up to?" I asked.

"I've just got back from Iraq for the last time. What a total shambles."

He looked like he'd had a bad time. I told him I was planning to go soon, once I was offered a position.

"For God's sake, don't do it. It's full of Walter Mittys. Most of the blokes I worked with I wouldn't trust them with a broom never mind a weapon."

He explained that many companies that were hiring would take anyone and wouldn't bother to check their military backgrounds, as they were manpower hungry for their big contracts. It was a wake-up call. I needed to rethink my plan. A company offered me a team leader job in Baghdad starting in two days. I didn't reply.

I didn't have to wait long before I received a positive phone call.

"Dom, it's Steve. I've an unarmed yacht escort job for you—Suez to Seychelles, leaving in three days. Are you available?"

"Do one-legged ducks swim in circles? Of course I am." The way to get security work was always to answer your phone and say yes to everything.

This was a godsend, as I really needed the cash. I told Titch to be on standby from the drop zone, Phil was still designing the kite boat around the Bosun dinghy hull, and I reassured Ang that we'd soon have some money coming in. Could the kite boat idea be back on?

I headed to Heathrow airport to meet my new partner, who I'd be riding shotgun with on the trip. It was to be the start of a great friendship. Nigel Watson Clarke, a fellow former Royal Marine, had spent years in Angola and Nigeria protecting the offshore oil fields. He'd been involved in some pretty punchy stuff, including being taken hostage after a huge firefight in Nigeria by MEND rebels and being held in the jungle for three weeks before being released. A true professional, we hit it off instantly.

We met the super yacht *Infatuation* in the port of Alexandria, Egypt. I love the hustle and bustle of Egyptian ports; it's a total assault on the senses: people constantly in your face, the noise of the mosques as people sing the prayers of the day, and the smell of delicious street cooking mixed with the stench of disgusting camel dung.

We waited on the dock as *Infatuation* slowly came alongside. Built in Holland by Jongert Yachts, she was a lovely 136ft sailing ketch with a dark blue hull and a white coach roof. We boarded and met Captain Reggie and the crew, along with an entourage of Egyptian port officials all lining up to squeeze as much money from the captain as possible.

The first part of the voyage was to navigate the Suez Canal. As priority was given to commercial shipping, we would be at the very back of the southbound convoy. The passage would involve five pilots coming on board to help navigate the yacht. Each pilot required a gift. The general rule of thumb was a gift of thirty dollars, 200 Marlboro cigarettes, and a T-shirt.

The canal is only one lane, so halfway down, ships have to wait at the Great Bitter Lake to allow northbound traffic to pass, and then the convoy continues. As one approaches the lake, there is a bend in the canal. As one looks across, it really does look as if the ships are sailing through the desert, and it is a sight I never tire of.

We exited the canal and headed south into the Red Sea. We needed to drill the crew on emergency procedures in case pirates ever approached us. The main area for piracy at the time was the Gulf of Aden. Pirates would commonly board yachts, steal money and equipment, and, in some cases, hijack or even kill the crew. A small number of cargo ships had recently been hijacked for ransom. Armed with a pump-action shotgun and rocket flares, our trip was uneventful, and we stayed as far off from the Somali coast as possible. We had one emergency as we sailed through the Straits of Bab el-Mandeb, a narrow strait that connects the Red Sea to the Gulf of Aden. Approached by three skiffs, we secured the crew to their emergency stations while Nige and I assessed the situation. Luckily, it was only fishermen curious to see such a beautiful vessel. Upon seeing me pointing a pump-action shotgun at them, they got the message and backed off.

I'd brought as much information as possible on kites so that I could use any time off watch to get fully up to speed and to decide which ocean to cross. I'd become totally absorbed in this new kite world and tried to think about what Phil's boat design would look like. I found it difficult to imagine how to rig kites to a boat, as I'd spent most of my adult life on conventional sailing yachts, such as the one I was now on. Kiting was going to be a very different proposition.

Crossing the Equator is always an event for any sailing vessel, as one must conduct the all-important "Line Crossing Ceremony." The Equator is the line of latitude that defines Earth's northern and southern hemispheres, and it is viewed as bad luck to cross without honouring Neptune, the Roman God of fresh water and the sea. The ceremony is an old tradition to celebrate any of the crew's first crossing of the Equator. "Celebrate" probably isn't the best description, as it normally involves the virgin sailors being tied up and having the galley food swill poured over them. It's all a bit of fun but an important tradition for sailors. It would be folly to head over the line without paying the proper respects; Neptune can be a very harsh and fickle god.

We arrived in the port of Victoria, Seychelles a few days after crossing the line. Captain Reggie and his wife, Catherine, really looked after us on the trip down. Nige and I went for a big night on the rum, exchanged details, and vowed to keep in touch. The following day, we said our farewells and headed back to the UK. The trip had given me a lot of time to work out the way forward.

As High as a Kite

January, Somerset, England

I'd decided that I would kite across the North Atlantic from Newfoundland to Exmouth, Devon and call the expedition "Kite Quest 200." All of my expeditions had "Quest" in the title in venerable recognition of Sir Ernest Shackleton's last expedition south on board the ship *Quest*. I added the "200" because 2005 was the 200th anniversary of the Battle of Trafalgar, and the UK had planned Lord Nelson celebrations nationwide.

Tempering my excitement at undertaking Kite Quest 200 was the fact that without attracting a big sponsor, kiting the Atlantic would be dead in the water. In turn, failure to get the expedition organised would likely mean us losing our home.

"We need to remortgage the house to get some cash in to see this through," I said to Ang. She didn't like it, but she agreed.

I was putting everything on the line for a venture that I didn't know would technically work. But to win in life, you have to take risks.

After a high degree of haggling, we managed to remortgage our home. I visited Phil to see how the design was coming along. Phil had some sketches, and we talked through how it could work, but this was new ground for both of us. We headed over to Exmouth to see Justin Adkin, who was building ocean rowing boats, to discuss the project. He kindly put Jamie Fabrizio on our build, and we talked about how long it would take to get the boat work done. We set a date of 1st of June. This would enable me to leave, depending on kite testing, in mid-June, thereby giving me a fighting chance of being on the right side of the North Atlantic before the big hurricane season started in earnest. I was still late, but I understood the risks, and so did Phil, who told Jamie that the boat needed to be strong enough to go over Niagara Falls.

I was having all sorts of problems learning kiting, the main one being that every time I went for kiting sessions, there was no wind. As much as I wanted to use Peter Lynn's kites to show gratitude for his support, getting them to work on the boat was a different proposition; it was simply too complicated to launch, and in offshore conditions, I deemed it unworkable with my current experience. If I didn't find a solution fast, I would have no option but to delay my plans and face financial ruin.

In an effort to attract further sponsorship, I'd been doing some publicity, and I was contacted by a publishing agent who was interested in my story. I met her in London, and she seemed confident about a book deal after the voyage. I left with a spring in my step. A book deal could be the end of my financial woes. I was not really bothered about being famous; most of my publicity was for the sponsors, and any book deal was purely and simply for money to survive. Titch had also received a phone call from a company called Kiteship. I arranged to meet the owner, Malcolm van Rooyen, in Exmouth with Phil. He had what he called an outleader kite, which had been used to power yachts. What I really liked about the kite was its simplicity: it had four lines and was very powerful, but it was much more controllable than the kite-surfing kites which were currently on the market. As a sailor, I could also relate instantly to its set-up, so I already had a rough idea of how to rig it. After a morning of flying the kites, we had a meeting about the best way to get the maximum power from the kite for boat propulsion. We needed to find suitable components to fly Malcolm's kites, so Phil and I scanned the catalogues of my sponsor, Burton Marine UK, who manufactured deck gear and rigging for boats.

As Phil and I drew sketches, I felt for the first time that I could actually pull this off. The downside to the outleader kite was that the main angles it could sail to were dead downwind or 30 degrees of 180 degrees, but Malcolm reckoned I could fly better angles with more practice. The predominant winds in the North Atlantic are generally westerly, so when it wasn't westerly wind, I would have to sit on the sea anchor, wait for the winds to change, and get kiting again. Rowing across the North Pacific with Tim, I'd gained a lot of experience of this kind of voyage of cat and mouse with the wind, and I knew it was a game of patience. A sea anchor is essentially a parachute on a 50m line attached to the boat, and it stops the boat capsizing in bad weather. I would never go to sea without one, and I always used Para Anchors Australia. I'd met Alby McCracken at the London Boat Show prior to rowing the Pacific. Apart from the water maker, it was the most used bit of equipment on the trip. He kindly gave me another anchor for Kite Quest 200. If we got into a hurricane, the sea anchor could be the difference between life and death.

Things were finally starting to come together—apart from sponsorship. I was struggling to sell this expedition, but with the tight time frame, I had to focus on the operational side of the expedition rather than spending time in funding meetings. I intended to start the voyage from St John's, Newfoundland, so I needed to visit to see what was available in the port and to understand the formalities.

St John's, the oldest and most easterly city in North America, is located on the very edge of the Grand Banks, which has been a place of fearsome reputation for sailors over the centuries. As a series of underwater plateaus, "the Banks" is relatively shallow, ranging from 33ft to 80ft and is not only home to one of the world's richest fishing grounds but also to winter storms, fog, icebergs, rogue waves, sea ice, and hurricanes. It also hosts the odd earthquake. A hospitable place it is not.

Sheer imposing cliffs that jut out into the bleak north Atlantic are the last I see of St John's. To the south is Cape Spear, the most easterly point of land in North America. Looking at the dark, foreboding landscape, I rename it Cape Fear.

This maritime community earned a hard living fishing on the Grand Banks. It'd be easy to imagine them as harsh and bleak like the surrounding headlands and treacherous ocean, but nothing could be further from the truth. People from Newfoundland are affectionately called "Newfies" and are quite simply the most welcoming and friendly people one could ever meet. St John's is also a Mecca for folk music, with live bands playing in the pubs most nights. They also produce their own rum called "screech." The Newfies in St John's knew how to make the best out of life. This was definitely my kind of town.

I linked up with fellow ocean rowers Nigel Morris, George Rock, Rob Munslow, and former Royal Marine Steve Dawson, who were, by chance, on standby to start their North Atlantic rowing record attempt. This was their second attempt. They'd tried, along with another ex-Royal Marine, Mark Stubbs, in 2002, but they had abandoned the row after losing their rudder in a storm. I knew Steve through his brother, Mick, who'd made a number of attempts to row solo across the North Pacific, which was recognised as the toughest of ocean rows. On his third attempt in 2004, he was capsized by a freak wave and rescued, but he'd vowed to return.

The screech flowed like water as we discussed their row and told old stories. For me, it was easy—I didn't have to leave by sea. The waiting to go was always the worst time on such ventures, and I could see the apprehension in their eyes; it would be the same for me when it was my turn. It was a successful visit, and the rowing crew gave me some good contacts in St John's to help me out.

Back in the UK, the boat build was falling behind schedule due to the extra work rigging the kite fittings and the other modifications I wanted added. Jamie was really committed, working around the clock. I was lucky to have him working on her. We also received a boost when a local businessman, John Welton, who owned a real-estate business in Taunton, came forward to sponsor us with cash. Things were starting to come together.

I really had to crank things up. The build completion had now fallen a month behind schedule. As I couldn't afford it to slip any more, I began spending more and more time in Exmouth in an effort to keep things on track. If everything now stayed on target, I'd have only two weeks for sea trials and kite sailing. This was a big call. I would know if the boat would definitely work only one week before she was being shipped to Newfoundland.

To add just a little more pressure, I noticed a press release issued by fellow ocean rower Anne Quemere announcing that she would be kiting across the north Atlantic in 2006. I checked out her website. Her boat looked really swept-up. Anne had a big following in France and rightly so. She'd also had more success at attracting big sponsors than I'd had. I needed to go this year. Looking at her boat, she would beat me hands down in a race across the pond. To be fair, she had cracked the technical part of kiting well before I had. I respected her for her ability to solve the puzzle of kites on boats, as it was a lot of work and commitment. But I had to be first.

Every boat needs a name. I'd been yacht racing for a Russian team for around three years. The yacht *Murka* was owned by a lovely couple, Misha and Olga White. I really enjoyed sailing for them, and the Russian crew were great shipmates. I rang Olga and asked if she minded me calling my boat *Little Murka*. She was delighted. She was also worried about me doing this trip and offered to cover the cost of my emergency equipment. This would be vital if I hit extreme weather.

This offer was even more resonant when I headed down to Falmouth to meet the rowing team I'd met in St John's. They were now on course to break the record for their crossing. TV cameras were there to greet their victorious row into Falmouth marina. They'd done a fantastic job. I tried to imagine what it would be like for me in the future when I would kite into Exmouth, the first to do so. I joined the team to buy them a drink to celebrate a job well done. They regaled me with their relief that at the start of the trip, they'd made a quick crossing of the Grand Banks. While it was a big night with many stories, I awoke in my car with only one ringing in my ears…

"I'm glad I'm not you, Dom, having to cross that beast now."

Big Roll of the Dice

June, Exmouth, Devon

It's June, and my boat is still in the yard. Jamie is working so hard on the boat that he's waking up in hot sweats. I'm pushing him really hard, and I hope he's hanging in there. Finances are getting tighter, and this is taking a toll on Ang as well. Things are far from happy in the Mee household. I'm starting to question whether everyone's going to burn out but me.

Finally, *Little Murka* comes out of the yard, and I do a few little jobs on her before she is lowered into the harbour in Exmouth. I take Hayley and Kieron, my niece and nephew, for a simple maiden voyage around the harbour.

It's time to see if this kiting concept actually works. To say I'm nervous is an understatement. I have a small outboard motor and head to sea on my own. I want to start the test out of sight of land. The last thing I need is the pressure of media cameras taking pictures of me while I struggle to fly these kites. I settle down a couple of miles offshore, have a cigarette, and start rigging the kite. I have an onshore wind blowing at around 12 knots (kn)[1]. I erect the mast, attach the kite, and start to feed the line out. The kite immediately fills but is erratic. I trim the kite in a similar fashion as I would trim a spinnaker. The rudder tiller between my legs, I point *Little Murka*'s bows downwind, easing the kite lines so that the kite sits above around 20ft in the air. I look behind me at the stern to see that we are moving: 1.5kn on the log; 2.5, 3.5, 4.0, the wind fills, and we increase to around 15kn. I feel like crying. It works!

The kite, however, needs constant attention. I cannot leave it for a second or it will collapse into the sea. I'm going to have to be on deck all day kiting. This just means it will be hard work, and I've never been afraid of graft. The feeling of relief is indescribable as I return to harbour. I go for a pint at the Ship Inn. The fisherman asks how my day is.

"Great! I've had a good day on the water," I say.

"Another pint, Dom?"

"Yeah, why not?" I deserved it.

This is day one of testing, with 13 to go. I decide to live on *Little Murka* in the harbour. Time on the boat is time well spent. It's a chance for me to get accustomed to the new boat and organise where everything will be stowed in the tiny 6ft x2ft cabin. As her dimensions aren't designed for a trip of such magnitude, nothing fits perfectly, including me. I'm 6'1".

Ang is happy with me being in Exmouth. It's been a pretty tense time building up to this point, and she needs a bit of time to herself. I also need time with my new mistress—*Little Murka*.

As much as the testing starts well, for the next week, there is not a breath of wind. On top of these woes, Phil is on holiday for the entire testing phase. I get in what testing I can, but it is clear that the 5m kite is not much good in any wind of 10kn or below. I ring Malcolm and tell him I could really use a bigger kite for light winds. Unsurprisingly, he's already ahead of me. He's already making a 10m kite for me, but it won't be ready for a couple of weeks. I'll have to test this kite in St John's. I want to cross the North Atlantic to test various kites in different conditions to apply to my ice boat in the future. It would also be the first expedition I would finish in England.

I think about where I am right now and the kites I have to test. It would be much easier to cross the mid-Atlantic route from the Canaries to the Caribbean. The trade winds consistently blow easterly downwind the whole way to the Caribbean islands. It would be a walk in the park for *Little Murka* and me, we wouldn't have to leave until December, and it would give us more time for testing. At the end of the day, I've set out my stall. My plans are made, there are expectations of me to undertake this trip, and the boat is being shipped to St John's in fewer than five days. I'm a very simple sailor; I have a boat that I can sail.

Let's get on with it and let the chips fall where they may.

We have one more thing to do—an official naming ceremony for *Little Murka* before we ship her to Canada. We hold the event in Exmouth, but I'm still unsure who should name the boat. I'd met Uri Geller by chance in London, and we'd hit it off. I'd told him what I was doing, and he'd loved it. I'd kept him up to date with progress.

I ask if he will name the boat for me. He is honoured and agrees to come down from Reading. There is a lot more to Uri than bending spoons. He was a paratrooper, was wounded in the Israeli six-day war, and was a big promoter of peace in the Middle East. Uri is a positive energy power station—he lights up a room when he walks in—and I have always found him a total gentleman. The team has a great day at the naming ceremony, and we all end up going to the Ship Inn for a beer. Uri amazes everyone; he even bends a military spoon. Top bloke.

It would be great to have a bit more time, but I know I can make it work. At the last minute, Iceland shipping line Eimskip kindly offers sponsorship. Its ships work throughout the north Atlantic between Scandinavia and Canada, and its benevolence is a real boost to the campaign. The ever-faithful Titch and I drive up to the port of Hull and put *Little Murka* in her container. En route, I can see something is on Titch's mind. I ask him what is wrong.

"Domster, it's not too late to pull the plug on this. This is pretty full-on, and I hate thinking about you out there at this time of year."

I reassure him that everything will be OK. I, too, have reservations, but that is par for the course; I'd be a fool not to.

There is nothing more for me to do other than prepare mentally for the challenge ahead and, of course, these awful farewells. Titch is not the only one who is concerned about the voyage. Ang has big reservations and is worried sick. I ring my mum and dad, and typically, they stoically take it all in their stride. "Good luck, son," Mum says before her familiar statement before I do anything dangerous. "I will get the prayer mat out again."

My younger sister, Sian, is cool about it; her big brother is off doing his stuff again. I know they are all worried; all I have to do is make sure I play it as safe as possible and come home.

"All the evidence shows that God was actually quite a gambler, and the universe is a great casino, where dice are thrown, and roulette wheels spin on every occasion."

- Stephen Hawking

It's Not the Size of the Dog

St John's, Newfoundland

I leave for St John's with a colourful collection of travellers, including Barry Roche and Louay Habib, who is the only Catholic Iraqi dry cleaner I know. We'd first met while sailing on Terry and Sue Robinson's Swan 48 *Assuage* about 10 years before and had remained friends ever since. We'd also sailed together for Team Murka. Like Titch, he's a little on the short side, but outside of dry cleaning, he was making his mark as a yachting journalist and offered to help get my trip out to the media. Louay and Titch are a comedy double act; it's great to have them along to take the edge off the wait. Barry and I sailed together on the Royal Marines sailing team. He'd left the marines to start a floor-cleaning business and was doing well. He's volunteered to come out and help buy last-minute items for the voyage, which is a definite help and, I guess for him, an opportunity to escape the fascinating world of floor cleaning.

The trip starts with us all drinking way too much in the Air Canada lounge, thanks to Neil Grunt Hunter from Air Canada Cargo, who had supported my expeditions to the Arctic. Despite the apprehension of the challenge ahead, the chemistry is so good between such close mates that we can't recall ever laughing so much. Thankfully, there are no TV cameras awaiting our arrival into St John's airport. We are definitely not looking corporate.

We arrive to a warm welcome at Leeside Manor, and I proceed to show the team around the hostelries and hospitality of St John's. After a couple of hours, it's clear that Barry has to go home, as I find him slumped in the toilets. The following day, after travelling around various chandlery outfitters to get the remaining equipment, we return to the Duke of Duckworth pub. Barry is adamant that he's never been there before. However, this is of no surprise; we call his unique view of life "the world according to Barry Roche."

"Hi, Barry!" says the waitress the minute we walk through the door. "I've been working in this pub for eight years, and you're the drunkest man I've ever seen."

It is pretty damning evidence, yet Barry still refuses to believe it.

Little Murka finally arrives. It's always a nervous moment opening a container. I've known people who have opened a container to find their boat smashed to pieces. But I have nothing to fear. Eimskip has done a great packing job. We take her out of the container and lay her on the dock for the final preparations.

I ring weather guru Mike Broughton. "How's it looking, Mickey?"

"I would sit tight. We have a hurricane forming off Cape Verde Islands. It's heading north towards Canada."

Hurricane Irene is the fourth recorded hurricane so far, and she seems to keep going. She's now lasted 14 days.

After two days of work, we decide on a "no move for five days" status due to Hurricane Irene still looming menacingly offshore. Irrespective of an outlying maelstrom, preparation continues, so *Little Murka* is lowered into the water. When we see her next to all St John's trawlers, we think she has been wrongly named; she should be called *Tiny Murka*. I test the new 10m kite outside St John's. It works well. She is ready to go.

The final item to put on the boat is my toilet, AKA a bucket. Whilst we are drinking, the guys spot a Corona beer ice bucket.

"That'd make a great toilet," says Titch, who is full of rum, a state that rarely makes for salient suggestions. "You can remember us when you're using it," he adds.

Equally full of rum, I agree. I don't really pay much attention to the practicality of the said bucket.

The Newfies of St John's are wonderful, and they rally around, helping us with anything we need. Eimskip lets us use its agent in the port, and this is invaluable to helping us to get things done. Some people look at me strangely when they see how small *Little Murka* is, but the fishermen don't bat an eyelid. They've seen this sort of thing before and still wax lyrical about Tom McLean, who has left a lasting impression in St John's.

I had the pleasure of meeting Tom on a number of occasions. An ex-SAS soldier turned sailor, if anyone owned the North Atlantic, it was Tom. He was the first man to row solo across the North Atlantic Ocean from St John's to Falmouth, England in 1969. In 1982, after leaving the army in a self-built boat measuring 9ft 9in, he set a new world record for sailing across the North Atlantic. His record was broken three weeks later by a sailor manning a boat with a length of 9ft 1in. Tom was having none of it, so he used a chainsaw to cut 2ft from his own boat, making it 7ft 9in long, and he sailed across again to regain his record. At 14ft, *Little Murka* is a cruise liner in Tom's world. Tom is a real gent, always giving time to people like myself who want to challenge the ocean. He is a true legend in the world of adventure.

We have four days to sit out the weather. Everything is ready, but we have no weather window because Hurricane Irene is coming through. The mariner's only possible solution to four days of boredom is rum.

It reminds me of waiting to leave Japan when Tim and I were about to row the North Pacific to America. Our hotel room was overlooking the surf. Even from our docile vantage point, it looked horrendous. We'd worked on the boat every day in Choshi Harbour, where they had 40ft sea walls topped off with another 30 feet of concrete blocks to keep the sea out. This community had built huge defences against the huge typhoons that would rip through every year. It was daunting. The North Pacific is the second-roughest ocean in the world, and we'd wondered how big the waves out there would get. It was this anticipation that made us hypersensitive to the massive task ahead. We knew we could die. We were tough guys, but the acceptance of the sheer enormity of the task was hard to bear. With such realisation comes fear, and emotions become raw. Even Tim, who isn't inclined to show his emotions, welled up on the night prior to our departure. And so did I.

I have great friends with me in St John's. It really helps me through this period, and we laugh so much that it actually causes pain. It's like going out with Jack D and Tommy Cooper all rolled into one as we laugh like there is no tomorrow—and perhaps there isn't. I guess if it's going to be my last party, we best make it one to be remembered and retold for years to come.

I need to check my satellite communication equipment to ensure it is working, so I head up to the top of the cliffs and set up. I dial into Peter Beardo at 7E communications to do a comms check. I patch through to Peter; the communications are working well.

"Do you know where you are transmitting from?" asks Peter.

"Yes, Peter, a hill in St John's," I reply, trying not to sound facetious.

He informs me that I'm actually transmitting from Signal Hill. On the 12th of December, 1901, on this very hill from where I'm transmitting, the first transatlantic wireless radio transmission was received by

Guglielmo Marconi. The message was wired from Cornwall to a receiver wired to a kite 400ft in the air. I feel the history, and I'm hoping to repeat it.

We've been waiting for the weather to improve for quite a while now. Louay has to crack some dry cleaning, and Barry has to return to polish some floors. We say goodbye in the pub where Barry collapsed on our first night. Titch and I are now alone at the bar in the "Duke." The party is over, and the moment of truth will soon be upon me.

We head down to check *Little Murka* to make sure nothing has happened overnight. It's a glorious sunny day with a nice offshore wind. The weather window from Mike is not open for another 24 hours, but it looks perfect.

"What about today?" suggests Titch.

I try to ring Mike but can't reach him. I look around the dock and see an old salt on a trawler. Who better to ask than a man who has worked all his life on this sea? With a big Newfie smile, the captain invites me to hop aboard. His trawler is in good shape, and as I walk towards the bridge, I think of the adventures this boat would have experienced over the years. The bridge is cluttered with charts and weather faxes as the captain is preparing for another voyage fishing for snow crabs.

The collapse of the northern cod fishery marked a profound change in the fishing community of Newfoundland. The 1992 moratorium banning the fishing of cod marked the largest industrial closure in Canadian history, and it was experienced most acutely in Newfoundland, whose continental shelf lay under the most heavily fished region. Over 35,000 fishers and plant workers from over 400 coastal communities became unemployed. The snow crab, however, was a lifeline for many Newfoundland fishing communities, replacing cod as a new source of income. The snow crab has a high value on the international fish markets, with most of the Grand Banks catches ending up on the tables in Tokyo and Beijing.

The weather fax noisily churns out another report. The captain studies it closely.

"How's it looking?" I ask hopefully.

"You should be alright. This wind is with us for three days or so. It looks good compared to what we have had over the last couple of weeks," he says in his deep Newfie accent, which sounds like a mixture of Scottish and Irish with a tweak of English all rolled into one.

The forecast is good and gives me enough time to clear the coast, as *Little Murka* can't sail against the wind. It would be disastrous if I were caught on a lee shore with the wind blowing me back onto the coast and extremely embarrassing to call for a rescue at the start of the trip.

I thank the captain. Titch and I exchange glances.

"OK, let's go."

It's game on. We dash back and grab the last pieces of equipment, pay the bill for the hotel, and in an hour, we are back on the dock. I climb into my Gul dry suit, descend the dock ladder, and jump into *Little Murka*. I slowly start rigging the 10m kite and double-check everything: radar plotter, navigation system, solar panels, and cigarettes. Two fishermen attach a line to my bow and start to tow me out. I give Titch a cheesy salute while he stares down nervously from the dock. I'm actually glad it has all happened so fast to avoid another grim "night before the voyage" scenario.

The wind is flunky as we exit the heads of St John harbour. I take a final look at Fort Amherst and Signal Hill, scanning to see if I can see Titch. With the winds behind me, the kite fills, and I am off into the wide blue yonder.

***

Titch sits on the headland as Dom passes behind the harbour wall. A blast of red punctures the horizon as the red kite fills with air. The tiny craft takes 30 minutes to disappear, confirmation to Titch that Dom is now on his own. With tears running down his face, Titch wonders whether he'll ever see Dom again.

"May the road rise to meet you.
May the wind always be at your back.
May the sun shine warm upon your face.
May the rains fall soft upon your fields.
And until we meet again may the Lord hold you in the palm of his hand."

- Irish Blessing

Kiting the Grand Beast

Grand Banks, Canada

My passion for travel and the sea started at an early age. From the age of 10, my favourite book has been the atlas. I used to pore over the pages, trying to imagine what the places and their people were like. This urge to travel was mostly inspired by my mum. Much to the protest of my grandmother, Mum was working at sea by the time she was 21, employed as an on-board medical officer on the cruise liner *Empress of Canada* of the Canadian Pacific Line. She visited Canada, America, and the Caribbean, and on her travels, she thankfully took many photographs. I remember first looking at her box of slides through a viewfinder and being truly amazed. Her travel pictures with blue skies and palm trees, taken in strange and exciting locations, brought my atlas to life. It was an education that I actually enjoyed. I didn't care much for the structured academia of school, preferring to look out of the window and dream of faraway lands and adventures. I left school and, at 17 years old, joined the Royal Marines to see the world. It had all brought me here to the infamous Grand Banks.

The land drops away slowly, and I actually feel better now that I'm out here doing what I've been telling everyone I am going to do. The dread of going is now over, and I'm in a positive mood. The 10m kite is working a treat, holding a nice course at around 7kn. *Little Murka* glides through the water with good trim. All the heartache I've gone through trying to make this work is over, and here I am, heading across the North Atlantic, bound for good old Blighty. I spot a grey whale breaking the surface just ahead of *Little Murka*—a Leviathan welcome to the Atlantic. A sea bird has followed me since I left St John's and remains with me during the day. I nickname him "Peter the Petrel." I take in a massive breath of distilled air. It's good to be back at sea.

The first days on solo voyages are generally the worst, as I try to get comfortable in my new environment, adjusting to my self-imposed exile. I have the added problem of coming down from probably the most intense drinking session of my life. We must have averaged two bottles each of Newfie screech a night. We'd enjoyed great St John's hospitality, but for the next two nights, the cold turkey demons will come to play. I never drink on expeditions; it's a danger element that I don't need. But there are small exceptions: I've stowed a miniature of Glenfiddich whisky to celebrate my 35th birthday.

I kite into the early evening, conscious that I must put as many miles as possible between the coast and me in case the winds turn foul. It's 21.00, and I'm totally beat, the stress of the last 10 days having caught up with me. The wind drops to nothing and offers me a chance to turn in. This is the first night I've spent at sea on *Little Murka*, and I'm rooting around trying to find things. The cockpit drainer is not working, so the foot well is full of water. I use my handheld bilge pump, which sucks in one of the kite lines and breaks the pump.

Great. It's just the start I didn't need. I'll try to fix it tomorrow.

The weather is calm. I don't set the sea anchor; I just collapse into the arms of *Little Murka* and sleep. The night demons come to taunt me, playing on my fear and paranoia. I toss and turn all night, sweating in my tiny space. It's an awful night.

I wake up with a 10-day hangover. I feel terrible. *Little Murka* is sitting beam on to the sea and rocking side to side. I hate the first few days; they're always horrendous: I have all this charged-up emotion while detoxing because I've been managing the fear with drink. It's technically referred to as a "shit fight."

In the rush to leave St John's, I did not stow items in the cabin properly, and they're all over the place. The wind has freshened to around 15kn. I stay in my sleeping bag and open the hatch. It's not a bad day; the sun is out with a little cloud. I fix my gimbaled cooker to its mount just outside the cabin door and start to get breakfast organised. Peter the Petrel is perched on the back of *Little Murka* making a sort of hocking noise.

"Morning, Peter. So you decided to come along?" I say.

"Honk, honk," he replies. I'm glad for the company.

Tim and I developed my diet prior to us rowing across the Pacific. It consists of a mixture of snacks and the UK military 24-hour ration packs. Breakfast is hot porridge, coffee, and a chocolate bar. Lunch consists of three pepperoni sticks, two packs of nuts, and two chocolate bars. Dinner delight is a choice of freeze-dried pasta with vegetables—pasta arrabbiata or my favourite chicken balti. On any particular day, on discovering that the evening meal would be balti, I would repeatedly shout "Balti! Balti!" in a suspect Indian accent. In ordinary circumstances, this action would be deemed stupid and childish, but when alone in the middle of the ocean, it is self-instigated morale.

The porridge starts to do its work and stirs me into action. I must also attend to my daily bowel movements, which, on expeditions, I can set my watch to. I go once a day at 08.00 to the minute irrelevant of what time zone I'm in. In a rum-induced cloud, my mates in St John's had persuaded me to bring the Corona beer ice bucket rather than the larger, well-tested Mark 1 bucket. It becomes clear that this was a rather stupid idea, and for the next three days, the boat stinks of urine. I need to devise a better solution. After 10 pints in the pub, ideas aren't generally the best. I remember one night down at my local village pub, The White Horse, I nearly bought a baby African ostrich after a few too many rums.

I take my time making preparations before I start to kite for the day. The first job before I exit the cabin is to put on my harness and clip on to the D ring just outside the cabin hatch. I do this every day without exception. If anyone falls over the side when not attached to the boat, they will die. It's that simple. The thought of being in the water watching *Little Murka* drift away is horrifying. The sea is an unforgiving and cruel place, and many sailors have been found dead in the water after falling over the side of a yacht; in many cases, the zippers of their waterproof trousers were open. A quick call of nature in the middle of the night costs many a sailor's life.

I rig the kite to the launch pole and then pump the rudder to point the boat downwind. I have four kite lines to control, and I steer the boat with the tiller between my knees.

"This would be a lot easier if I were a spider," I say to myself.

I'm slowly getting the kite to fly near the boat to get it moving, and as I pick up speed, I ease the kite lines out to around 30ft from the boat. This is not the end of the job, as the kite needs constant trimming. I can't leave it for one second, or it will collapse. I'll have to stand all day on the deck to successfully fly the kites, and this is what I'll do. It's not particularly comfortable standing for 10 to 15 hours a day, but it's easier than rowing, and we do more miles kiting. The day passes, and the 10m kite flies well. I see a humpback whale, which breaches right in front of the boat. It is such an amazing creature. I have seen many whales on voyages, but they never cease to fill me with awe and wonderment.

When Tim and I were mid-Pacific, we rowed right up to a large sperm whale resting after a deep dive. We rowed nervously towards this 60-ton beast which could smash our row with one swipe of its tail. As we came alongside the whale, it turned on its side to look at us through its big black eye. I can't explain how it felt, but this creature seemed to look inside my very soul. The whale knew we weren't a threat and swam right under our boat before showing us his fluke as he dived below the waves to hunt the giant squid in the abyss. It's a moment I'll never forget.

The weather is good, with a 12kn breeze accompanied by a small following swell. I have to admit that I'm enjoying the kite sailing, and I am making reasonable speed. I decide that I'll kite from first light to last light and sleep on the sea anchor for the duration of the voyage, as kiting is highly stressful on the body and mind. It's a good start to the voyage, but I'm still nervous: the Grand Banks is an unpredictable place, and I won't feel safe until I'm in deeper water.

> "O'er the glad waters of the dark blue sea,
> Our thoughts as boundless, and our souls as free."
> - Lord Byron, *The Corsair*

First Punch

I wake to grey skies and a bigger swell, but they're all in a favourable direction for my voyage to England. I want to get going as soon as possible, as I'm mindful that I'm still on the Banks, where life will be very difficult, especially if I encounter a serious storm. This is my first objective, and based on my current mileage per day, I should be clear in under a week. I launch the 10m kite, and it powers up instantly. *Little Murka* leaps to life. There runs a 7ft swell, conditions that give me a good chance to see how *Little Murka* performs. The boat is fully laden with food and water for 60 days, supplemented with 10 days of emergency rations, so I'd managed expectations on her performance with all the weight on board. I start experimenting with the kite height to see what distance would give me the best speed. The 10m at 20ft seemed to be the sweet spot. Combining my life as a member of a yacht-racing team with my surfing experience, I start to really work the boat in the swell. I'm really surprised by how well she is performing, surfing around one in three waves, and despite her size and shape, she's a pretty quick boat. The one thing that puzzles me and gnaws away at my mind is that the waves are densely packed together. I'd expect more of a gap, known as the fetch, between each wave. Here, the gaps are extremely short, so I can really work the boat as hard as I dare in these early stages.

The wind has been building all day, and I am struggling to hold the kite, so I need to change down to the 5m kite. I've been thinking this manoeuvre through all day and running the drill through my mind. It helps that I've worked on the foredeck of many racing yachts over the years. The key is to do it fast, as the boat would go beam on to the waves, and as I now have a 10ft swell running, there would be a high probability of capsizing. I depower the kite from the tack line at the bottom and bring it onto the cabin roof. With four quick bowline knots, I have the 5m kite launched in about five minutes. It feels good that I'm starting to gel with the boat, and my kiting is improving by the minute. The 5m kite has other ideas. It is far more difficult to control than the 10m and is very lively. Scampering around to my front like a naughty child, it creates an even more intense mental and physical workout. When I ease it out to 30ft, it starts to behave a little better.

By late afternoon, the breeze has picked up to around 25kn. I need to be conservative, so I stop kiting two hours early. I wait for a lull in the waves, as I'd have to drop the kite and launch the sea anchor immediately to avoid being capsized in the swell. I move at a furious pace and it's done. I feel more confident and slightly more in control after a day kiting in these moderate conditions, but I am still apprehensive about what lies ahead; the infamy of the Grand Banks makes me wonder if this newfound confidence is warranted.

The wind picks up after my evening meal. I go on deck to ensure that the sea anchor is setting OK, and my anemometer states the wind as 35kn. Peter the Petrel is off the stern, paddling behind the boat. I settle back into the cabin; it seems as if every five seconds, the boat is being hit wave after wave after wave. The swell has built to a steep, fast wave with a very short fetch. It's nasty. I don't sleep well. I don't want to think about what it would be like in a full gale.

I wake the next morning. Kit is all over the cabin from the bumpy night. It's obvious, but I think it anyway: *I need to get more organised.*

It's a gloomy day outside, but the Southwesterly wind direction may be workable for kiting. I rush through my breakfast. The one thing last night told me was "Get off the Banks—and quick!" We start kiting, but the sea state is all over the place, and the wind is very temperamental. It's clear that the wind is about to change, and not in my favour. I battle for three hours in an attempt to make progress, but I'm fighting a losing battle, and the winds are strengthening Southeasterly. I can't hold the kite at that angle. I'm forced to get back on the sea anchor. The sea anchor is my first line of defence in storms. It is a parachute that enables the boat to face the waves; the parachute helps the boat to grip the water to avoid being capsized. With the line attached to the bow of *Little Murka*, I submerge the parachute and pave it out to 50m. I used one of Alby McCraken's para anchors in the Pacific, and it saved our lives. We encountered three typhoons and several severe tropical storms on the voyage, but our sea anchor held firm, so I'm confident it will work here.

The wind outside has been building all day. I'm in for another rough night. I ring Mike Broughton for a weather update. It's always good to speak to Mike. He's a born sailor, and we've raced together over the years for various teams. We first met in the military, where he was captain of the Royal Navy sailing team. I joined the team, along with fellow Royal Marine George Hendry, for the Royal Navy sailing challenge to Australia. The Royal Navy had a very experienced sailing team at the time, and they decided it would be a great challenge to test their skills against the best yacht racers in the world. A campaign to participate was organised to enter the Southern Cross race series in Sydney, followed by the hardest offshore yacht race in the world—the Sydney to Hobart.

The Sydney to Hobart Yacht Race is an annual event which is hosted by the Cruising Yacht Club of Australia. It starts in Sydney, New South Wales on Boxing Day and finishes in Hobart, Tasmania. The race distance is approximately 630 nautical miles*(nm). The race is run in co-operation with the Royal Yacht Club of Tasmania. One of the many factors that makes the race so difficult is the Bass Strait, and the waters of the Pacific Ocean immediately to its east are renowned for their high winds and difficult seas. Although the race mostly takes place in the Tasman Sea, the shallowness of the Bass Strait and the proximity to the race course means that the fleet is very much under the influence of the strait as it transits from the mainland to Flinders Island. Even though the race takes place in the Australian summer, the "southerly buster," a weather system which is specific to the southern hemisphere, can create winds of up to 50kn in as little as 12 hours. I prefer its other common name—"The Big Bust." Whatever the name, these storms often make the Sydney-Hobart race cold, bumpy, and immensely challenging for the crews. It is typical for a considerable number of yachts to retire, often at Eden on the New South Wales south coast, which is the last sheltered harbour before Flinders Island. The yacht race gave me my first exposure to heavy-weather offshore sailing. This chance encounter with Mike was to take my life in a new direction. Going to Australia gave me my first chance to compete against world-class sailors from around the globe, and it was a sport I pursued to become a future professional sailor.

I represented the Royal Navy at the Southern Cross regatta on a Nelson Merrick Farr 43 called *Quest*. I was the last crew member to be selected for the RN team, but the boat was too small for a full crew for the Sydney to Hobart. I had to get another ride. I put an advertisement on the CYC yacht club notice board: "Royal Marine grinder, grinds like ten men, needs a ride to Hobart."

I was lucky enough to be selected for Team New Zealand on one of the smallest boats to do the race that year—a Hick 35. This was to be my baptism into heavy-weather sailing. We were hit early by a southerly bluster. On day two of the race, we had five "knock downs," which describes when the winds are so strong that the yacht is knocked flat. I woke up underwater, not knowing what was happening. I clambered up the yacht to get clear of the rigging and saw that the captain had gone overboard and was floundering in the sea. The quick-thinking helmsman managed to get a line on him as he went over, thereby preventing us from losing him. The yacht recovered slowly, and we got back in the race. I heard over the radio that 10 boats had retired. The question was, as one of the smallest in the race, were we going to make it to Hobart? The yacht was built just prior to the race, and the toilets had not yet been fitted, so we had to do our toileting over the side. This was not only unpleasant but also pretty dangerous in high winds. Yet, these extremes were the reason I fell in love with yacht racing. I was hooked. We made it to Hobart and won second in class—a damn good result. Mike and I became great friends during the campaign in Australia, and he opened the door to some great sailing opportunities for me.

Mike has bad news. "It's not great, Domster. It looks like easterlies are in for the next five to six days. You're going to have to ride it out on the anchor."

This wasn't what I wanted to hear. I had to get off the Banks as soon as possible.

Mike continues, "At its worst, the wind will be up to around forty knots, possibly higher in the gusts. There's a very complex weather system forming in the south."

***

Thousands of miles away in the forests of Ghana, Bebearia Barombina butterflies are trying to find mates. Intense activity ensues as males defend their perches, while females fly down a jungle flight path, seeking suitable males. This small beating of their wings starts meteorological alchemy, as if created by Yemaya, the African sea goddess herself.

Several weeks later, the minor perturbations of the butterflies influence the formation of a tropical wave—a small trough of low pressure that drifts across the Atlantic Ocean towards the Caribbean. Meteorologists in the US later number this trough tropical depression 10. The fledgling storm dissipates on the 18th of August, just 10 days after forming in the Gulf of Guinea. Yemaya has not finished with her magic; as the weather system breaks up, it forms another depression, which develops into a complex storm system tagged as tropical depression 12. This witch's cauldron of weather is going to create a monster which will carry the anger of Yemaya like no other storm. On the 25th of August, system 12 becomes a goliath category 5 hurricane. They call her Katrina.

New Orleans is trying to evacuate all residents under a mandatory order issued by President George Bush. This is fine for those who have the means to get out, but for an estimated 100,000 people on a low income who have no cars and don't even have enough cash to take a bus, there is only one option: the New Orleans Super Dome, which is the shelter of last resort. The stadium has previously been used as a shelter built to withstand 200mph winds. At 06.10 on the 29th of August, Katrina makes landfall with the power of a nuclear bomb and wipes out southern Louisiana.

Hurricane Ally

On the sea anchor, *Little Murka* is taking a beating. The conditions have worsened, and the waves are unbelievably fast. I've never experienced waves like this in all my years on the ocean. In Pacific typhoons, the waves are huge but with a longer fetch. At one point, I am on deck, wanting to witness nature's power. *Little Murka* rises over the top of 50ft waves and then descends to the bottom of a huge valley before the next mountain of water carries us up again. It really is akin to being on a moving mountain range. I see many so-called rogue waves out there; I'd guess that every two hours, I'd see one massive wave tower above the rest.

The complex weather system Mike refers to is now a full-blown hurricane heading across the Gulf of Mexico towards New Orleans. I listen to my shortwave radio as warnings are issued to the gulf coast of America. I'm glued to the "Voice of America" broadcast. The National Hurricane Center's director, Max Mayfield, warns federal officials in Washington DC of a nightmare scenario should New Orleans' levees not hold. Winds are smashing windows in high-rise buildings, and floods are wiping out large swaths of the Gulf Coast. The National Weather Service office in Slidell, which covers the New Orleans area, puts out its own warnings: "Most of the area will be uninhabitable for weeks… perhaps longer," and it predicts "human suffering incredible by modern standards."

On the sea anchor, I have little else to do but listen to what's happening; I am, after all, inextricably linked to events happening down south. I'm pretty scared. I understand weather. This is a massive storm—maybe the biggest ever. I am north of it on the ocean. I'm going to be affected by it, whatever happens; the only variable is how badly I'll be hit.

"Balti! Balti!" Finally, some morale in hell's kitchen.

I can't believe what I'm hearing on the radio; it is apocalyptic. I recall when rowing the Pacific with Tim, we listened to the world service when 9/11 happened. For us, isolated from the world, it felt like Armageddon. We'd had visions of landing in America after our row and it being like *Planet of the Apes*. Alone at sea, the world becomes much smaller. While the landscape is massive, with an unreachable horizon, the remoteness means that my world revolves around the intimacy of my 14ft craft. With no constant media bombardment, life is simple, yet there is a feeling of being cut off, alone, and forever living in a state of survival. When I hear news like that coming out of New Orleans, I feel fearful because of the sheer scale.

The radio booms out in my cabin: "Where's George Bush? Where's George Bush?" I continue to listen in horror as law and order breaks down and despair rules in New Orleans. The biggest superpower on the planet, one that has fought wars all over the world, cannot help its own people; it's shocking. For the "withs" in America, life is good, but seemingly, no one gives a damn about the "withouts."

New Orleans is on its own. The Super Dome has become lawless; there are reports of rape, murder, and crack dealing. God help those families trying to live through this nightmare. I try to sleep, but it's no use, and I lie awake scared about what is happening outside my tiny world.

When day breaks, I ring Mike. I am still in the storm and continue to be hit constantly by the tempest seemingly trying to claw its way into the boat.

"Dom, it's carnage out there. Katrina has broken up and is sending out hundreds of violent, smaller storms like a car bomb in Baghdad. All major weather systems have been affected. Unfortunately, you're in for bad winds for another five days."

"It's pretty bad out here," I say, which is the understatement of the year. I don't really want to know the answer, but I ask anyway, "Will the winds increase any more?"

"In three days, it's going to blow hard—forty knots plus. Sit tight. We should see easterlies after the tail end of Katrina."

I hang up. It's incredibly important on voyages of this nature to keep a positive mental attitude. Maybe the worst is over? Katrina is a big one. We tend to get one or two per season. If this is the beginning of the end, then I should get good winds to get me to Exmouth. I'm keen not to hang around in this land of giants.

In the angry, foaming sea outside, Peter is paddling like an athlete in training for the seagull Olympics. I settle down with my iPod and listen to *The Tales of Moby Dick*. As I hear the tale of the white whale, I smile as I remember having the privilege of seeing a white sperm whale in the Pacific.

In this onslaught of the waves, I think *Little Murka* is feeling the strain as the storm increases in power, as Mike predicted. I'm worried that the boat is going to break up due to the sheer violence of the Grand Bank wave train.

I ring Phil Morrison. "Hi, Phil. I'm taking some pretty bad hits out here. Do you think the boat will hold up?"

"Yes, the boat will be fine. Don't worry about that." Phil's tone is matter of a fact; he doesn't sound at all hesitant.

I have a quick word with myself. "Get your shit together, and stop flapping."

On board, I am starting to have some equipment problems. My sat phone isn't recognising my phone antennae. Luckily, over the years, I have received great support from comms guru Peter Beardow. I'm not getting too stressed, as I know that Peter will find a solution. The dampness of the cabin is playing havoc with the electronics. I have one tin of Inotec MS1000 waterproofing spray, which is starting to be the most important bit of kit on the boat. I just wish I had a couple more tins. The spray clears all the water from the electrics, aiding the total recovery of every piece of equipment it's sprayed on. It's the reason I call it magic spray. I've used Inotec products on all my expeditions and have found them invaluable.

Remarkably, despite the weather, Peter the Petrel is still with me. I have become quite attached to my feathery ocean companion; I'll miss him when he decides to go.

The Grand Banks is horrible. Huge waves are now accelerating in every 10 seconds at a very steep angle and hitting *Little Murka* with the power of a large truck. Because they're so vertical, we go straight up the face, where I see only a dark foreboding sky before me, then slam straight back down, where all I see is the wrath of an angry ocean. It continues unabated. I pray for the winds to ease. I'm not ashamed to say it—I'm terrified.

I awake feeling dreadful. All night, I've been thrown around the cabin, and I feel as if I've been in a 12-hour rugby maul. Thankfully, the violent actions of the boat subside by first light. I look out of the hatch; the winds have finally eased, and the sea has calmed considerably.

Thank God.

I've made it through a nasty storm, and despite my doubts, *Little Murka* has taken the pounding in her stride. The wind has swung around; time to get kiting again and get out of this horrific place.

The wind is light, and we kite with the 10m full, moving along slowly at 3.5kn. It's not much, but every mile is getting me closer to escaping the Grand Banks, and my life depends on getting clear. I've already taken a beating in 40kn; I'd hate to think what it'll be like in a hurricane. I'm in no mood to find out.

Peter still follows me. He flies ahead to settle on the water, waits for me to pass, and then flies ahead again, playing his own little game. In my isolation, Peter is a real comfort to me.

I think of all the people back home: friends, family, and Ang. Love is a powerful force, and it is driving me hard. Strip away all the sponsorship, danger, and adventurous spirit, and this trip is about a guy on the ocean just trying to get home.

In the first two weeks, I've covered only 130nm. At this average, it will take me 180 days to reach England. It is a sobering thought. I have supplies for only 60 days.

"Truth uncompromisingly told will always have its jagged edges."
- Herman Melville, *Billy Budd*

***

The initial hope that an early start to the annual hurricane season would mean an early finish now seems a little optimistic. Hurricane Maria, like Irene, is a Cape Verde-type hurricane that forms in the mid-Atlantic in September and tracks to the northwest, strengthening as it moves over warm waters. She's the thirteenth named storm, sixth hurricane, and fourth major hurricane of the record-breaking season. The storm reaches its peak and is graded as a category 3 hurricane. It is heading north towards the Grand Banks.

Hurricane Nate is also forming behind Maria and is heading to the north Atlantic. The Canadian Navy ships heading south to the Gulf of Mexico to support the relief effort in New Orleans find themselves in the path of two deadly hurricanes. *Destroyer HMCS Athabaskan, Frigates HMCS Toronto*, and *HMCS Ville de Quebec* set a course straight down the middle of the two weather systems. They experience heavy seas and slow down to a snail's pace as they battle through the high waves. They are carrying vital supplies to relieve the suffering of the inhabitants left behind in Louisiana.

Hurricane Ophelia is also forming behind Nate. This erratic hurricane, which is graded as a category 3, careers up the east coast of America. She is also en route to the Grand Banks. Three major hurricanes are heading north. The hurricane factory of 2005 is at full production.

Russian Roulette

The kiting is going well, but the wind is dropping throughout the day. I try to keep focused to keep the kite flying. Mentally, if I can get off the Banks, I know I can make it home. My satellite pager has been beeping nonstop for the last two hours, but because of the light winds, I have kept my launching mast up to help the kite fly.

It's probably Titch trying to set up a radio interview, I think. *I just don't have time for that right now.*

The sea is flat calm for the first time since I left St John's. The wind dies slowly, and the kite drops to the deck. I sit on the deck and finally enjoy the moment of calm after so much violence has been inflicted on me by the ocean for the last 10 days. It's beautiful. Five dolphins arrive and swim around *Little Murka*. I sit, feeling totally at peace. I lie on my back and look up to the sky. I see streaked cirrus clouds, and there's big wind on the way, but for now, all I want is to be in this moment. The break will allow me to vent the boat, dry all my gear for tomorrow, and get back in the game. I leave the launch mast up and ready the kite just in case the wind fills back in, and we can snatch some more miles home. The wind does not return, and I daydream. I am snapped back to reality by another beep from my pager. I better check it.

"DOM, STOP MOVING ANY FURTHER EAST. HURRICANE MARIA AHEAD. STOP MOVING. MIKE B." A full-blown hurricane is on the Grand Banks. It doesn't get any worse than that. I sit and contemplate. I need to be ready, but I also need to speak to anyone back home in case this goes badly. The odds aren't great, but I'm determined to do my best. My Iridium sat phone is working again, but I don't use it so that I can save the battery. I can use the Mini-M to call, as the weather is so flat that I should get a signal. I can't reach Ang, so I call Tony, my father-in-law, and brief him on the situation. Mum and Dad, Louay, Baz, et al. are now briefed. All I can do is sit and wait for it to hit. I clear the deck to make storm preparations. From nowhere, four big waves hit *Little*

Murka, sending her reeling. In shock, I grab the guard rail to steady myself. I watch the four waves continue north, and I look back to see if any more follow. Nothing. That was it. Were they the four horsemen of my apocalypse? I set the sea anchor and make my battle preparations: eat well and early to bed. I will need all my strength for this one. I sleep with all my emergency equipment nearby before closing the hatch for the night.

I call out to Peter, "It's going to be dogs off chains tonight, Peter. Hang in there."

I've had the best night's sleep of the trip so far. There has been nothing all night, and the sea is still flat calm.

OK. It's running late, I think. *At least in the daylight I'll be able to better gauge how bad the storm will be.*

The pager beeps. It's Mike: **"WHAT ARE THE CONDITIONS AT YOUR LOCATION?"**

I flash up the Mini-M and dial Mike's number, anticipating bad news, as has been par for the course since leaving St John's.

"It's flat calm," I explain.

"That's great. Another fifty miles east, you'd have been in hell. It looks like you've dodged a bullet."

The relief is palpable. A colossal weight lifts from my shoulders. But, on this trip, it couldn't just be good news.

"Hurricane Maria is heading to Norway, but we have another Hurricane, Nate, in the south along with another hurricane behind it, so expect to be on the sea anchor for the next few days. It's chaos weather-wise. This season is unprecedented; I've never seen anything like it."

I sit down on deck and enjoy the calm. It's not going to last, but I'm safe for now.

"Honk, honk," says Peter, sensing my mood.

"We're safe for today, Peter." I throw him a brown biscuit. He's not impressed. Clearly, UK military rations are not his thing.

I get busy throughout the day, trying to repair my equipment. It's always an uphill struggle with boats, especially small ones. We are only 80 miles from getting off the Banks and the drop off the continental shelf into the deep water of the Atlantic. This trip has been really tough. I've hardly had any kiting days due to the bad weather. *Little Murka* is starting to malfunction piece by piece, and I'm trying my level best to keep all the systems online, but it's only a matter of time before I start to lose major equipment to the further storms ahead. I pray for no more hurricanes. I've been playing Russian roulette so far with the weather; I just hope my luck holds out. I can't believe another two hurricanes are behind Maria.

What the hell is going on?

While working on deck, I hear the noise of a helicopter, and all day I've been hearing a low industrial humming sound. I check the chart. The only thing it could be is the world's largest offshore oil refinery 100nm to the south of me. I can't believe I can hear the hum from the facility.

The Hibernia oil platform is the world's largest. It needs to be. It is located in one of the world's roughest stretches of ocean. The platform sits on the ocean floor approximately 260ft deep with its topsides extending approximately 160ft high out of the water. The platform acts as a small concrete island with serrated outer edges designed to counter icebergs. Production commenced on the 17th of November, 1997. A dedicated fleet of shuttle tankers continuously operates between the platform and the mainland. The crew consists of 280 people who spend three weeks on the platform and three weeks on land, flown to and from by helicopter. So, I guess I'm hearing a crew change. It's rather comforting knowing that I'm not too far away from other humans out in this wild ocean.

The oil industry learnt the hard way about the violent weather conditions on the Grand Banks during the early days of exploration on the Hibernia field. Ocean Ranger was designed and owned by Ocean Drilling and Exploration Company, Inc. (ODECO) of New Orleans. This $120-million semi-submersible rig was hailed as unsinkable and the pride of ODECO's offshore fleet. Ocean Ranger was the largest rig in the world. The size of two football fields and towering 35 storeys, it was the symbol of stability designed to work in the heaviest sea conditions. At the start of its operation, the rig listed badly due to a ballast control problem, but luckily, the sea conditions were calm, and the problem was corrected, but it set the scene for disaster. On the 14th of February, 1982, the Grand Banks was experiencing a violent storm of 90kn winds and 50ft-plus waves. At 20.00, a gargantuan wave smashed through a porthole in the ballast control room, causing the system to short-circuit. This was the worst thing that could happen. All hell broke loose. The ballast tanks sit below the surface and control the entire stability of the rig, a system that was now completely malfunctioning. Two other semi-submersible rigs were also drilling nearby: the Sedco 706 at 8.5 miles northeast and the Zapata Ugland at 19.2 miles north of Ocean Ranger. Both were experiencing 55ft waves and 100kn winds. Ocean Ranger contacted both rigs to discuss the ballast problem, which was now out of control. In 30 minutes, the port ballast tanks filled, causing a 10-degree list on the rig in the face of storm-force winds and seas. The crew of the unsinkable vessel tried hard to gain control of the situation but, due to flaws in their training, did not have the knowledge to fix this rare problem. Around an hour earlier, the nearby Sedco 706 experienced a large rogue wave that damaged some items on deck and caused the loss of a life raft. Soon after, radio transmissions were heard from Ocean Ranger, describing a broken porthole and water in the ballast control room, with discussions about how best to repair the damage. Ocean Ranger reported experiencing storm seas of 55ft with the odd wave up to 65ft.

At 01.00, the crew made a distress call and started to evacuate the Ocean Ranger. The lifeboats were not designed for this kind of emergency, and only a fraction of the crew made it to the muster stations. It was chaos. The rig capsized at 3.15 am. Most crew members were in the freezing water, wearing only their clothes and life jackets. The lifeboats had failed to launch, tossing the crew into the raging sea below. The Atlantic Ocean in February would have debilitated the men the minute they hit the waves below, the shock of the cold water would have been the first thing that hit them, and hypothermia would have set in almost immediately. *MV Seaforth*, the first supply vessel that came on station, tried desperately to reach 20 of their shipmates who were in the water. Due to the horrendous conditions, when lines were thrown to the men in the water, they barely responded. They simply could not hold the lines; their hands were unable to operate due to the onslaught of hypothermia. The entire crew of 84 men died in the water that night, reinforcing the morbid irony that the *RMS Titanic*, also described as unsinkable, also perished in nearby waters.

The following day, a Russian container ship, *Mekhanik Tarasov*, which was 65 miles to the east of the Ocean Ranger, was struggling with the conditions. *Mekhanik Tarasov* listed dramatically after being hit by a series of huge waves before sinking. Only five crew members survived. In 24 hours, the Banks had taken 116 souls to add to the long list of mariners who had fallen to this hellish outcrop.

It is on this hellish outcrop, in my tiny 14ft dinghy, that I face the outfall of Maria. The only things to look forward to are days of strong headwinds and bobbing about in huge seas. In the storms outside my life on board is miserable as my body is wedged into a 6ft x 2ft rocking and rolling cabin. I lie flat on my back and stare at the ceiling of the boat. I try to sleep as much as possible, if only to stop the unbearable boredom. I've been trying to learn Russian on the trip so that I can better communicate with my Russian teammates on racing yacht *Murka*. I also have books, but with the delays so far, I've read them all. I have a number of audio books on my iPod, and my main source of news is via shortwave radio. I'm so close to the edge of the Banks that I feel very frustrated and hopeless. I've been out here for 26 days and have spent 90% of my time stuck in this tiny cabin. To add to my incarceration on the Banks, I check my Garmin GPS. I'm in an eddy being driven south further onto the Banks towards the Flemish Cap. I'm at my lowest moment to date. It feels like I'm never to leave the Banks.

I can't believe my bad luck on this trip. Getting sucked further into the main part of the Grand Banks is a bitter blow; it could be an extra three days of kiting to get off now. Morale is really low, and my mind is getting darker. The Banks doesn't want to let me go. It's just another kick in the teeth on this wretched ocean. The Flemish Cap fills me with fear; it was the last area fished by the FV *Andrea Gail* before she was lost at sea in the perfect storm. I worry about what the three hurricanes will produce just for me—another perfect storm? Only this one won't have the Hollywood treatment. This is a living nightmare.

"Billy's at 44 north, 56 west and heading straight into meteorological hell."

Sebastian Junger, *The Perfect Storm*

Into the Abyss

I've had my share of tough voyages over the years, but this crossing is tougher than I could have ever imagined. It is hell. I'm now on the sea anchor, drifting south into the main area of the Grand Banks. At my lowest ebb on the voyage so far, I find I've run out of cigarettes. I foolishly decided to give up at the behest of my wife, Ang, who thought it would be a good idea to give up on the trip. I'm really not in the mood for giving them up; smoking is about the only bit of morale I currently have.

The Grand Banks is hitting me so hard that I'm really struggling to keep it together. I can't go forward, and I can't go back; I am totally trapped. I can't see any way out of this situation. It's hopeless. To add to my despair, I now have to go through nicotine withdrawal. All I want to do is smoke my arse off.

I talk to my video camera to download my emotion. I remember from my solo kayak through the Arctic that the camera almost became a friend, a therapist with whom I could offload my worries. I'm a tough character, but I choke up as I speak. I can feel my throat becoming harsh as fear, anguish, and hopelessness sear my eyes with tears. I question myself. I've learned the hard way, having served in the Royal Marines for 15 years, but all that experience is no help to me right now. I am stuck on a tiny boat, living in a 6ft x 2ft coffin-in-waiting, unable to do anything to change my circumstances. In my darkest hours at night, the boat feels like a tomb, and the sinister Grand Banks is now controlling my destiny. I fear it's going to keep me forever as another trophy of its destructive power.

The winds are picking up and again, and we are being battered by waves which are intent on destroying us. I try my Mini-M phone. It has stopped working. I revert to my trusty Iridium handheld sat phone. It has also malfunctioned. I have no voice communication with the outside world. The only communication I have is by Mini-C, so I can at least send email messages. My satellite pager is also working, so I can receive messages from Mike but can't reply.

I'm starting to lose it. As I am in the cabin alone, the boat, which is under constant battering, is starting to fail. I'm now becoming more and more aware that as much as I'm feeling the mental strain, *Little Murka* is feeling the physical strain. Every hour is a battle to keep all of her systems working. Everything is starting to malfunction, but thankfully all is still workable... but for how long I'm not sure. I continue to be drawn south, further into the Banks. I receive a page from Mike: **"LOOKS LIKE YOU HAVE A FAVOURABLE WEATHER WINDOW FOR THE NEXT 24-48 HOURS."**

I prepare. This is the first chance in the last five days that the winds have blown the right way to get me closer to home. I switch on and check the conditions. We have around 20kn of wind with a sizeable swell of around 15ft. In my mind, I'm trying to be conservative, but I know I am going to have to push it today; I've got only 50 miles to get off the Banks, and I can get out of this eddy which is driving me south.

I don't like the conditions. The sky is angry, and the wind is going to build, but I have no choice. I quickly retrieve the sea anchor and then immediately pump the rudder to point *Little Murka* downwind. In this wind speed, I can use only the volatile 5m kite. This should be fun. The wind bites the kite and tries to rip it from the launching mast. I look behind nervously at the large following seas under the heavy, menacing clouds. The kite powers up but is difficult to control. I steer the boat carefully with the rudder between my knees and try to get into the groove. *Little Murka* is doing 8kn as we build speed on the crests of the waves that break behind the boat. I settle down. The boat is now averaging around 10kn, and I'm feeling more confident. If we can maintain this speed, we'll be off the Banks in five hours.

The weeks of frustration start to emerge as I'm kiting. I feel angry and reckless as the wind increases. Now, the waves are getting bigger. Within four hours, I am experiencing 30kn gusting 35+. I don't care. I'm out of control. I hate this ocean.

"Is that all you've got? You're nothing!" I howl into the wind, tasting the salty spray that showers me.

I push the boat harder as if I'm on the final leg of a world championship race. In this sea state, a 40ft yacht with a full experienced crew would be very weary. I'm on a 14ft dinghy carving up the waves. I'm out of control. I'm dangerous. I know it deep down, but I can't stop. I put my iPod on and put "Vertigo" by U2 on repeat. The heart-popping bass lines make things worse. This voyage is stretching my sanity.

I surf down 20ft waves. I feel like Laird Hamilton, the world-class surfer, conquering the biggest waves in the world. *Little Murka* is flying. I just wish I could see this from the air or someone could get a photograph. I'm intoxicated by adrenaline and anger. I'm leaving the Banks alive or dead. A big wave breaks behind the boat, and we are catapulted down the wave. I scream in exhilaration and fear. I can barely keep *Little Murka* in a straight line down the wave. I look at the speed: we are doing 14.5 knots. The boat is maxed out on speed. I see the bow of the boat driving underwater. We are going to flip right over. To avoid an imminent disaster, I throw my weight out of the back of the boat and hang on with my legs clenching the guard rail as I try to bring the bow back up. It works, but we wipe out, and a second wave breaks on the boat, nearly washing me over the side. Even though I am clipped on, it's a close call. I'm not fazed; I'm still too angry, and I'm not giving up that easily.

"I'm not fucking done! I'll tell you when I'm fucking done!" I scream at the sea.

I launch the kite, and we are off again. I'm amazed that we can even be out in these conditions; I'd never have believed it possible. I crank the iPod up and try to hear the music above the storm: "Uno, dos, tres, catorce! Turn it up loud, Captain, lights go down it's dark, the jungle is your head."

"Come on, bitch!" I scream at that cold-hearted Atlantic woman as we punch off the top of a huge wave.

The high wind sends salt water to cut my face, but it only drives me harder. The cockpit is full of water as we surf the boiling ocean. I'm totally possessed but totally in the zone. This is total insanity.

"Hello, hello, I'm at a place called Vertigo."

I'm struggling to hear Bono as the storm gets louder, trying to get into my head and send me back to the Banks. I drive harder; *Little Murka* is being pushed beyond what she's designed for, but she takes it again and again. I'm leaning off the back of the boat, hanging my full body weight to stop the bows going under as we hurtle down the face of 20ft-plus waves. I don't know how this storm is going to end, but I am going out with a fight. I've been kiting for around six hours; the storm is full force at around 40kn. I look behind me to see the most monumental wave of the day. It's frighteningly huge. I go for it. I pull in the kite, and then a big ease gives me more speed. I launch off the top of the beast as it arches steeply and then breaks, with tons of foaming water surrounding us as we go down the face as if fired by a cannon. I am totally out of control.

"Shit."

We career off to port and broach on the face of the wave as it breaks. The angry white water throws me off the boat like a rag doll. *Little Murka* goes onto her side. She's going to capsize. She comes back up as the wave passes like a freight train.

All at once, my sanity takes over: *Get a grip. You're going to die.*

I climb back on board and immediately deploy the sea anchor to get stability.

"OK, I'm done," I say sheepishly to the giants of the Grand Banks.

I return to the cabin exhausted. I can't believe what I've done today. I settle down and, in the best British tradition, have a cup of tea. I take stock. The GPS shows we are now on the very edge of the Banks and are out of the south-moving current. This is a great result, and it has invigorated my confidence that I can conquer this wretched ocean, but it's cost nearly everything.

New rule: No more U2 on deck. Sorry, Bono.

"For there is no folly of the beast of the earth which is not infinitely outdone
by the madness of men."

- Moby Dick

The Demon

Living in such a small space with the constant pounding of the ocean means I'm struggling to remain lucid or sometimes even function. I try to sleep, but the cumulative stress on my brain causes me to wake up when the dreams tell me that something has gone wrong. In these conditions, things will fail because you know something's going to fail. I just hope it's not the sea anchor.

The seeming hopelessness of the situation battles my commitment to see things through, which is something I've always done no matter what. Yet, the enormity of my task is stacked against me and is tearing me apart. My emotions are like the peaks and troughs of the waves that are constantly throwing me around. I'm riding a very fragile roller coaster; one minute I'm buoyant, and then I'm hitting rock bottom. I'm trying to keep it balanced somewhere in the middle. It's so difficult and, sometimes, really unmanageable. I've got to try to get it together. If I don't, I'm not going home.

The wind eases overnight. As it's still in the right direction, I get up early to set up. The wind is around 10kn, with about a 10ft swell running. I need to keep going. After so much adverse weather, I've covered only 400 miles. I need to start rationing food, as my 60-day voyage is looking more like 100 days. The waves calm throughout the day, and the wind slowly drops to nothing. I've kited for 10 hours. As I drift along slowly, I see two small sharks on the surface and nearly run them over before they dive beneath the waves. I've reached a meeting of currents—the cold Labrador current from the north and the warm Gulf Stream from the south. This meeting of cold and hot water is always abundant with fish and predators. I settle down, stow the kite, and put the kettle on. A pod of six pilot whales swims past, followed by a large pod of dolphins. As the remains of the swell gently rock *Little Murka*, I feel safe again.

Peter is still with me, despite the weather and the madness. It's strange; he doesn't really get anything out of this relationship other than a perch at night, so why does he stay? Whatever the reason, I'm glad he's here. My SeaMe radar beacon sounds the alarm inside the cabin. We have a ship nearby. The radar beacon acts as an early warning for me. We are so small that no big ship will see us, so the beacon activates an alarm when it detects a ship's radar, giving me an opportunity to get a visual on the ship and contact them on VHF to let them know where I am. There are many cases of yachts being run down by big ships at night, and it is an even bigger hazard for *Little Murka*. The scariest part of being run down by a ship is that they'd have no idea it's happened.

Unfortunately, Tim and I had been in a collision on the ocean during our Pacific row. We'd been rowing for 136 days and were just 1,000 miles from making landfall on the west coast of America. Having rowed for five months, we were both fatigued, but morale on board was good. I was on watch when we rowed into an offshore fishing area. I'd seen a number of long liners fishing a few miles off during the early part of my three-hour shift. I'd seen a fishing boat maybe half a mile away, so I'd stopped rowing to observe the intentions of those on board. There was a 10ft swelling running, and as the vessel approached, it steered sharply to starboard by around 50 degrees, so I thought it had seen us and steered away. I kept an eye on the vessel, as something wasn't right. The vessel then started to turn back onto its original course with another big 50-degree swing. I tried to reach them on the radio. No response. The deep sea fishing boat was now heading directly towards us. As the boat bore down, I was transfixed, like a rabbit in the headlights, until I saw our fate. I looked at the bridge windows of the vessel; nobody was at the wheel.

"Tim, get out!" I yelled.

Seconds before the impact, I dived over the side. I swam as deep as I could and waited for the propellers to slice me into chunks. I thought I was going to die, and I accepted it. To my surprise, I surfaced along the side of the boat. I saw two fishermen hauling in their lines oblivious to what had just happened.

"Stop the boat! You've run us down!" I screamed in horror.

I then found myself in the middle of hundreds of hooks trailing off the back of the fishing boat. I swam clear, but my main worry was Tim. The fishing boat finally stopped about 600m away. I started to swim to get to Tim, but it was extremely difficult due to the sea conditions. On finally getting to our boat, I found Tim treading water outside the cabin. The fishing boat *Judy S* had struck *Crackers* amid ships, lodging her on the bow and driving her underwater with Tim trapped in the cabin. It was a terrifying ordeal. I was so relieved to see

Tim alive, and that was all that mattered. We tied a line to the now-capsized *Crackers* from the *Judy S* to bring her back up to salvage the equipment. The row was over. *Crackers* had finally righted, but I was in the water with another swim of about 400m to get to the *Judy S*. After three hours of rowing and the swim to reach Tim, I was exhausted. I looked at the fish lines that had fish jumping frantically on unattended lines and then noticed blood was being pumped out to sea from the hold of *Judy S*. It struck fear into me; for the first time on the trip, I thought about my ultimate fear—sharks. I nearly didn't make it to the *Judy S*, as I had no energy left and was paralysed by the fear of being taken out by a large shark. I collapsed on the deck. It was not the ending anyone had wanted, but we'd survived.

I scan the horizon and pick up a small tanker ship coming into view around three miles away. The tanker slowly approaches *Little Murka*. I repeatedly call the ship up on VHF channel 16; it stops around 100m away. I explain over the radio that I don't need any help; it would just be nice to talk to someone. I get no reply. Since the satellite phones went down six days ago, I'm only able to speak to Peter… and myself. Cured of their curiosity, the ship moves off, and I return despondently to my evening meal, looking over a beautiful sunset with Peter. During the voyage, I've been updating my blog for friends and family. Peter the Petrel has turned into a minor celebrity. My local pub in Somerset, The White Horse, has been debating what species of bird Peter could be. They eventually discover what he is; however, "Peter the Northern Fulmar" doesn't have the same ring to it. He'll always be a petrel to me.

The night is calm, so I sleep well. The morning brings a very light easterly breeze that I will try to use. I set up and pump the rudder to bring *Little Murka* around. During this operation, just as I'm starting to fly the 10m kite, I hear a large splash behind the boat. It must be one of the dolphins from last night. I turn and smile. To my horror, it's not a dolphin but a huge great white shark. The shark is huge at around 14ft and is only 10ft off the back of *Little Murka*. I'm completely gripped by fear to the point where I cannot move. My pulse is racing into overdrive, and I'm close to hyperventilating. The shark has always been my demon, and now it's here. Its presence has invaded my whole body: my nervous system… my brain… my blood. I'm shaking. A commando I may have been, but out here, a green beret means little. I daren't look at it, but at the same time, I need to see what its intentions are. The shark is wallowing gently behind the boat, dorsal fin exposed, enhancing all of those nightmare scenarios I've imagined from the movie *Jaws*. I never in my wildest dreams thought I'd see a great white out here. I can't get back in the cabin, as the launching mast is in place, but I feel so exposed on this tiny deck outside. It's horrible. My nemesis has finally come for me. After 10 minutes, I'm still trying to consider what to do. The pace of the shark hasn't changed, and I have a flare pistol in my pocket. I consider firing it at the shark.

My mind shoots back to my solo trip to the Arctic, it being the last time I was confronted by a dangerous wild animal. I was on foot. Due to the ice conditions being so bad that year, I couldn't proceed by kayak. An angry musk ox, a kind of Arctic bison, armed with large horns and a very bad temper confronted me. It ground its hooves into the dirt, shook its centre-parted horned head, and glared at me aggressively. I decided to take the first step. I unslung my pump-action shotgun and fired a warning shot. The musk ox, rather than being dissuaded by my escalation of force, decided to attack. The beast charged me at full speed. I fired, reloaded, and fired again. It still kept coming. I fired my final shot at point-blank range. The ox charged relentlessly over the top of me, cracking four of my ribs before taking off into the hills, leaving me in the dirt in total shock.

I decide not to aggravate the shark. With one flare in the pistol, I'm outgunned on all fronts. I decide that the best thing is to not move, sink down, and pray. I keep glancing back to see the shark's next move. I look at its cold black eyes. They show no emotion—just death. I'm utterly at its mercy as it monitors my every move, assessing if it wants to attack. The shark sinks below the surface and is gone.

I daren't move for another 30 minutes, as I'm paranoid that it's still somewhere near me. I assure myself that this is an encounter that I'll never forget, and as far as overcoming my fear of sharks, it's only given it a true form. I can't purge it from my mind.

I drift slowly in the light wind before the wind swings around and is, once again, against us. I deploy the sea anchor, but I daren't put my head over the ocean just in case my demon is around. It could pop up at any moment and bite my head off. In my fragile mental state, the shark's presence isn't helping. Thanks a bunch. The only upside is that it hasn't eaten me.

Once more, the ocean rages. Mike sends me more bad news via pager. I know Mike wants to give me good news, but there just isn't any. The BBC world service crackles with reports of Katrina. New Orleans is still suffering. I reflect as I hear these awful stories. How can such despair be permitted in a country that claims to be a superpower? The situation is terrible for the people in Louisiana. I wonder if it would be different if the hurricane had landed in Texas, George Bush's state. I guess we all know the answer to that, but as Louisiana is predominantly a black state, it doesn't seem to matter as much to the powers in Washington DC. I find this situation shameful, and my heart goes out to the people stranded without hope.

Their situation takes my mind wandering to when I served in Iraq in 1991 after Operation Desert Storm. The Iraqi Army turned its venom on the Kurds who, at the behest of the US, fought against Saddam Hussain's army. The US abandoned the Kurds, who, in turn, faced the full force of the Iraqi Army and were slaughtered in droves. The Kurds ran to the safety of the mountains, but the journey had a high price. I arrived in one of refugee camps on the border with Turkey. It was a heartbreaking scene with around 500 people dying daily. As a young man of 20, it was a sight I would never forget, and my recollection bears this out as I now think of the cloak of death that covered their camp. The situation is similar to that of other people without hope—the people in New Orleans.

After three days on the sea anchor riding out another small storm, I have another chance to head east towards home. The day is grey with some fog. It'd be a pretty depressing day in other circumstances, but for me, a day moving east is always a great day. Sailing in the fog is always weird. It's a bit like walking around in a dark basement: I'm never sure what I'm going to come across.

It's the 17th of September, which is "Crackers Day," the date that Tim and I were run down four years ago. I kite through the fog, and just off the starboard side, I'm greeted by a sperm whale. This is very appropriate on "Crackers Day," as during our row across the Pacific, we'd been privileged to encounter sperm whales regularly, including an ultra-rare white sperm whale that we kept a secret so as not to put it in danger from Japanese hunters. I've thought of Tim most days on this trip. I miss him on this one. After six hours, the wind changes, so depressingly, I go back on the sea anchor.

> "You're going to need a bigger boat."
> - Chief Martin Brody, *Jaws*

***

In West Africa, Yemaya has concocted another tropical wave, sending it across the Atlantic. This little sister will grow into one of the most powerful hurricanes ever recorded. It will trigger 90 tornados and activate the largest evacuation in US history. The National Hurricane Center will call her Rita. In this game of Russian roulette with extreme weather, Dom's luck is about to run out.

Death Sentence

On board *Little Murka*, my Mini-C satellite system is starting to break down. The green light keeps extinguishing, which means that the Mini-C isn't receiving satellite information. Mini-Cs never break down. This system is found on most ships travelling the ocean, as it's the most robust system available. The Mini-C gives me weather information and email, and right now, it's the only remaining communication with the outside world. On this trip, the storms have been so violent that I'm worried that the ocean has damaged the antennae. The green light comes on. I hastily plug my laptop into the Mini-C and send an email to Ang: **"Don't worry. Comms down. This may not work again."** I press SEND. Thankfully, the message goes out. I receive a Mini-C email from Ang: **"Hang in there. I love you."**

I lie down to try to sleep, but the storm is pretty bad. It's only meant to be about 30kn, but we have a lot more wind. I'm noticing with a certain degree of angst that over the last three days, the seas have been building. The waves are now around 25ft to 30ft, and the wind meter is recording 40kn in the wave troughs. My GPS is starting to malfunction, and my electrics are suffering badly due to condensation.

I'm busy working on the electrics, dismantling all the systems to coat them with MS1000 protective spray to purge out the moisture. The roar approaches like a freight train, and before I can react, a wave slams the boat, its force pushing us to near vertical, and then breaks on top of us. The sheer violence throws me through the cabin door and onto the deck, which is awash with the roiling sea. I quickly dive back into the cabin to avoid being washed over the side. It's huge out there; it's one of many massive waves that dance menacingly around me. This particular monster has breached the hatch, and *Little Murka* is flooded. I'm desperately trying to keep the electrics alive. All my systems seem to be malfunctioning at once, including my SeaMe radar.

The big wave that hit the boat has taken its toll and really spooks me. I feel very scared. I go out from my front hatch and check the sea anchor. My two back-up carabiners have been sheared off. This only adds to my fear. If we lose the sea anchor, I'm doomed, but it seems to be hanging in there. I put another carabiner on to back up the sea anchor line. I return to the cabin and sit down. I then break down and weep.

For the past few days, we've been taking hits nonstop, pinned down in a 40kn northwest gale. These are the biggest seas I've seen so far. The waves are smashing me every 10 seconds. They're so vertical that they whack us straight up a wall of water and then straight back down. There's no time to get my bearings before it starts up again.

Surely, I think, *it must be almost over.*

I've never seen anything so unrelenting.

Wiping my sleeve across the glass of the hatch, I peer out into the storm. Where there used to be peaks endlessly swelling and falling, the waves are now starting to break. This isn't good. A set of breaking waves can easily capsize a boat. The first one knocks you off course, the second sends you reeling, and the third rolls you over. The second one hasn't hit us yet, but it's coming. With my comms down, all I have is Mini-C messaging and maybe not for long. I might have only one chance. I've got to speak to Mike. This storm is way stronger than what was forecast. Mike is one of the best tactical navigators alive. If he can't help me, no one can.

At 17 years old, Mike was the youngest sailor in the disastrous Fastnet Race of 1979, where 15 of the most experienced sailors in the world died in brutal 60kn winds. Since then, he's built an unequalled reputation among yachtsmen as a weather guru. Nobody knows how to manoeuvre through nasty weather better than Mike.

I send him an urgent text and then try to steel myself while I wait for his reply. It'd be fantastic to hear a friendly voice, but with my sat phones down, that's going to have to wait. It'll have to be via the pager. I know it's a long shot, but I have nothing else.

In all the years I've been a Royal Marines Commando, from the war zones of Belfast to Iraq, trapped by polar bears on a glacier in the remotest regions of the Arctic, and rowing the Pacific during violent tropical storms, nothing has been as terrifying as this.

This time, I'm scared to the core.

"We can easily forgive a child who is afraid of the dark; the real tragedy of life is when men are afraid of the light."

- Plato

* * *

Mike and Louay have been sharing a house in the Hamble, living in post-divorce bliss. The house is located on the edge of the village, just five minutes' walk to the marina, and, more importantly, five minutes to the pub. The Hamble is the home of many racing yachts and crews from all over the country and is, in essence, the centre of the universe for UK yacht racing. The car park is full of all manner of exotic automobiles owned by the rich and famous who moor their yachts at Point Hamble Marina.

Mike has just arrived back from the Maxi Rolex Cup in Porto Cervo, Sardinia. Louay is in the kitchen. The TV is on, with George Bush trying to explain why no help has arrived in New Orleans: "I understand the anxiety of people on the ground, so there is frustration. But I want people to know there's a lot of help coming."

"Hi, Mike. How was Sardinia?" Louay pours himself a large Mount Gay rum; it's Thursday after all.

"Pretty good, thanks mate. It was pretty breezy this year," Mike says with a big smile, nodding in response to the president's address.

"I got a call from Titch yesterday. He was asking about the weather for Dom. Has he spoken to you?"

"Yes, I spoke to him briefly at Rome airport. It's my next job." Mike opens up his laptop on the kitchen table and goes to put his sailing holdall into his room. He returns, opens his weather software package, and scans the north Atlantic. He sees an email come in from Dom's Mini-C unit:

"SEA STATE UNMANAGEABLE. FIND. ME A WAY OUT. I'M CRYING BLOOD MATE."

For Dom to say he's crying blood... thinks Mike as he shakes his head. He can hardly believe it. Dom is the last person he'd ever expect to send such a message. He'd always considered Dom a hugely determined and very courageous guy. They'd first sailed together in the Sydney-Hobart race in 1996. Since then, they'd been to hell and back: all kinds of races, hideous sea states, and monster waves. Mike had never once seen Dom scared.

Feeling tension in his gut, he moves quickly to his computer to check the charts. He knows that whatever's happening, it must be horrendous. He knows he has to give the best advice he's ever given. His friend's life is at stake.

"What's it looking like?" Louay cranes his neck to see the screen.

"I'm still waiting for the latest weather updates to load, but I've just received this message from *Little Murka*. Take a look."

Louay reads Dom's cry for help. His blood runs cold. He tries to be upbeat. "Maybe he's having a bad day and just sent it at a low point," Louay says lamely.

"Dom's been having a bad day since he left St John's," Mike replies as the weather data fill his screen. He plots Dom's last known position and slumps in his chair. He can't believe what he is seeing on the screen. "Louay, pour me a very large Mount Gay…"

Mike has never seen anything like it. Hurricane Rita is roaring through the Atlantic. Days ago, she'd started as a tropical storm over the Turks and Caicos Islands. Moving steadily towards the Florida Keys, she'd managed to harness 150 km/h winds, putting her at category 2. She's amped things up considerably since then. What Mike now sees is a death sentence.

Not three weeks earlier, when Hurricane Katrina devastated the Gulf Coast and laid waste to New Orleans, she was listed as the fourth most powerful hurricane on record. But now Katrina has been bumped to fifth, because Hurricane Rita is stronger. Both are ranked at category 5, with winds in excess of 250 km/h. Category 5 is the most extreme hurricane force known to man. There is no category 6.

Appalled, Mike drops into his chair and stares at the satellite images. He's looking at chaos—winds from every direction and completely unpredictable seas. He can only imagine the waves. He rings Titch to update him.

"Titch, it's biblical out there, and Dom's in his little dinghy-with-a-lid-on, riding seas far worse than the ones we faced at Fastnet. I don't see how he can survive. If the violence of the waves doesn't tear the boat apart first, he'll be hit with winds 10kn greater than what he's in now. He must already be facing absolutely horrifying conditions—huge seas with 60kn winds gusting up to 70kn. At his current position, Dom hasn't even seen the worst of it yet."

Titch shudders just thinking about it and thanks Mike before hanging up. Trying to stay calm, he thinks back to when he'd sat on the harbour wall in St John's, wondering whether he'd ever see Dom again. It may have been a prophetic thought, as he knows the waves created by a 60kn wind are not twice as violent as waves from a 30kn wind. They're 25 times as violent. Facing 70kn winds is catastrophic. He decides not to tell Ang.

Knowing Mike needs time alone to solve the problem, Louay decides it's time to go down to the pub. "I'm heading to the King and Queen. I'll shout you one in."

"Give me an hour. I want to look at some other weather models to see if there's a better outlook for Dom."

The weather forecast for Dom runs through Louay's head as he sets off down the cobbled street. He'd been through heavy weather before, but never 70kn. That would be unmanageable in *Little Murka*.

He and Dom had been so inseparable on the racing circuit that they'd been nicknamed "Twins" after the 80s movie starring Danny Devito and Arnold Schwarzenegger. The fact that Dom may not make it back this time is a hard pill to swallow, yet he knows that if there's anyone who can make it, it's Dom.

He enters the King and Queen, and his popularity means he is greeted warmly by the usual suspects. Acky, an old acquaintance, is holding court, offering anyone with a willing ear another tale of bravery upon the high seas, and Finley, as usual, has allowed his good nature to get him roped in to helping behind the bar.

"Usual, please."

Finley can already recognise that something is troubling Louay "So, what's happening with Dom? He hasn't put anything on his blog for a couple weeks," he says casually. He'd known Dom from working as his mast man on many yachts.

"He's lost his communications in all the storms."

"Ah, that'll be why then," Finley jokes, already refilling the pint glass that Louay has quickly emptied.

"So what's his ETA to the Scilly Isles?" Acky butts in.

"I don't know." Louay stares out of the window, not really listening to the conversation. He's brought back to reality by the amber nectar waved in front of his eyes.

"You're miles away, shipmate. What's up?"

"It's Domster; he's in a terrible storm off the Banks."

"He'll be alright, Shippers. It's Dom; he's been through worse." Finley takes a big gulp of beer.

"That's the problem; he hasn't. He's been in fifty-knot winds for a couple of days, and there's seventy knots on the way."

The King and Queen is a sailors' bar. The silence tells its own story.

Mike scans through all the weather models in the hope that he's wrong, but he finds the same inevitable truth staring right back at him. He casts his mind back to 1979 when he was racing in the Fastnet race.

The 603-mile race, which goes from Cowes, Isle of Wright to Fastnet Rock, south coast of Ireland and finishes in Plymouth, is a gruelling offshore race, but in 1979, it turned into a fight for survival. A severe storm descended onto the race area. On day three, the storm hit the fleet at full force. By the end of the day, it was carnage: 75 yachts had been capsized and five had sunk. The largest peacetime rescue operation was launched by the Coast Guard and the Royal Navy. Fifteen sailors and three rescuers perished in the vicious storm. Mike was 17 then, and it remained burned into his memory.

The storm heading towards *Little Murka* is far worse.

After a decade advising world-class yachtsmen and adventurers, Mike has never had to send such a foreboding message. He has to tell Dom, but the news is so grim.

After he writes the message, he hovers over the key before he hits SEND. It may be the last message Dom ever reads.

> "Perhaps they are not stars in the sky, but rather openings where our loved ones shine down to let us know they are happy."
> — Inuit saying

Dark Spiral

It's all taking its toll. *Little Murka* is showing the strain. So am I.

I can't explain the helplessness I feel. I click on the world service to try to escape, only to be reminded that Rita is causing havoc in America and is heading my way. I'm struggling to manage as we are, never mind with the fallout of another hurricane on the back of this storm. I pray again. I can't seem to escape the feeling of hopelessness. I do a video diary, which normally helps, but it only adds to my despair; I just can't shake it. To add misery to my anguish, I have no comms. Mini-C is dead.

It's a horrible feeling knowing that I won't be able to contact anybody. No-one on Earth will have any idea where I am. I feel like I'm on the moon, far from home. I'm still only 500 miles from Canada. I'm trying to work out how I'm going to proceed. I need to start rationing food today and looking at a rainwater collection.

The only option available is to carry on kiting. If I see a ship, I'll get them to relay my position to Titch. Hopefully, they'll be more responsive than the last ship I met. Even in this darkness, I think of seeing the Scilly Isles and how life will be so much better. I've just got to hang in there. Right now, I'm just falling apart at the seams. I've never been like this before. I feel embarrassed as I weep. I feel pathetic.

The seas are giving it to *Little Murka*, but she's a tough little boat, shifting and bobbing like a lassoed calf while the parachute anchor strains underwater to keep her bow pointed into the waves.

For me, the mental battle is the worst part. If I can't get a grip on my thoughts, I won't be ready to act when Mike sends a solution. I'm going to need the presence of mind to pull up the sea anchor quickly and launch the kites. There may not be a moment to spare.

Meanwhile, I've got to distract myself and restore some frail sense of normalcy. If I allow myself to freak out, I could miss my window. Beneath the light of my head torch, I prop open a book and try to pretend it's just another storm.

"My dear fellow," said Sherlock Holmes, as we sat on either side of the fire in his lodgings at Baker Street, "Life is infinitely stranger than anything which the mind of man could invent…"

In the infinite darkness outside, howling winds roar against us, shoving great, huge swells beneath my starboard side. As *Little Murka* falls forward, the book nearly flies from my hand. The light on deck extinguishes ominously and then flickers back on. My stomach muscles tighten, bracing me, as if I expect to be slugged in the gut. Long moments pass before I realise that I'm holding my breath.

What's that noise? It's a deep groan. *The ropes of the sea anchor creaking?*

"If we could fly out of that window hand-in-hand, hover over this great city, gently remove the roofs, and peep in at the strange things going on…"[i]

Another groan from the deck. The book doesn't drown out my worry. I don't like the sound of it.

Tossing the book aside, I squint through the hatch. So much spray is washing over the boat that it's difficult to see, but it looks like that sound is coming from the trip line. I peer harder, and I see something I've never seen before in all my days of heavy weather sailing—the sea is pulling the trip line so tight that it's delaminating the deck around the cleat. If the trip line fouls around the parachute anchor, it'll collapse the parachute. I can't let that happen.

Alarmed, I don my head torch and stagger out into the swirling, pitch-black storm. It's clear the cleat won't last much longer. Once it's ripped from the deck, the trip line will tangle in the parachute. If we lose that, there'll be nothing to hold us in place. We'll be at the mercy of the waves.

If I cut the trip line and there's a break in the weather, I'll have to pull the 50m anchor line out of the water by hand while the waves try to yank it back. It'll be a vicious tug-of-war. It could take hours. We could miss our window and be stuck in this hell. While considered, it's an agonising choice, but I can't risk the lines getting tangled in the anchor or ripping off the cleat. I have to jettison the line. I'll deal with the consequences later.

Standing ready, I wait till we drop to the bottom of a 60ft trough, where the pressure is lowest, but there's still so much load on the line that as soon as I release it, the boat starts to spin around, knocking me left and right as it turns. I grab the gunwales to steady myself, but it's too late.

Up behind me comes the surly growl of a monster wave, rising over us, and there is a massive explosion as it smashes down onto *Little Murka*. I'm catapulted through the slightly open hatch. I crash against the cabin floor with such force that I wonder if my shoulder is broken. My thoughts are reeling.

How could that wave come up from behind?

It's so chaotic out there, it's difficult to work out what's happening. I know one thing—we are in one hell of a storm.

Picking myself up off the floor, I force the hatch closed, check my aching shoulder, and curse. It's like being beaten by a gang of cowardly thugs in the dark when you can't even see who they are. At least, with the trip line free, I'm hoping we'll sit better in the storm.

I feel something I've never felt before. I can't quite place it at first. It's then that I realise that we're listing starboard. I feel like we're side-on to the waves. That's impossible with the sea anchor.

Grabbing the head torch, I rush back on deck. The monster wave must have spun the boat fully 360 degrees. To my horror, I see that the spin has wrapped the sea anchor rope around the keel. The parachute is fighting the waves on a short, tight leash. It can't manoeuvre, so it's actually holding us beam-on to the waves—the worst position imaginable. In these conditions, one breaking wave will drag us up to the top of the crest and then flip us, end over end, all the way back down. We won't stand a chance. At any moment now, the torque alone could rip the keel off and put a massive hole in the boat. If that happens, we'll sink like a rock.

With the waves pounding across the bow, I brace myself on the deck and pump the rudder with all my might. But no matter what I do, the sea strikes back, pummelling the deck with enormous volumes of water. Again and again, I'm forced to abandon the rudder to bail out the water before I can go back to the rudder. It's hopeless. I'm getting nowhere. I'm losing control of the situation. I'm fearful of what's going to happen.

And then the unthinkable happens. The sea anchor rope snaps.

Stunned, I watch in utter disbelief as the line breaks and disappears into the dark. Black waves suck it down into oblivion as if it never existed at all. It takes a fraction of a second but feels like an eternity. We are moving quickly into a new and even deadlier phase.

The waves, towering over us, now have new meaning. Moments ago, they were only our enemy. Now they are death. With the sea anchor gone, we have no defence.

This is getting ridiculous. A part of my mind won't face it. I can't lose the sea anchor. It never happens. It's a fluke, like the engine falling out of a trawler.

"A ship without an anchor…"

That's what people say when someone's lost… without hope…

I can feel myself sliding into shock.

Come on, Dom! Think!

Losing the sea anchor… well, OK, that's serious. But it could be worse. It's not as bad as ripping off the keel.

That's right, it could be worse. Get it together.

But we're in the craziest of seas. Without a sea anchor to hold us into the weather, what will happen to the boat? Will she slowly point upwind by herself? Or will she just roll and roll and roll? I have no idea. I've never been in a situation like this before. I've never even heard of it. All I know for sure is that the two worst disasters in modern sailing history were the result of boats without drogues or anchors.

The first was the 1979 Fastnet disaster in which Mike was involved as a boy. The second was in June of 1994. Twenty-one crewmen were rescued from the sea when a storm hit 35 boats on the way from New Zealand to Tonga. Three crewmen disappeared completely. The rescue boats found nothing but an empty life raft with an activated emergency position-indicating radio beacon (EPIRB).

Since those disasters, every sailing manual warns:

When you're faced with gale winds at Beaufort Force 10, there are only three viable survival tactics:

(1) Running under the stabilising control of a single drogue
(2) Running under control with a series drogue
(3) Riding out the storm with a sea anchor.

Without that, your chances of survival are next to nil.

We are at Beaufort Force 12. We don't have a drogue. And we've just lost the sea anchor.

"Hell is empty and all the devils are here."
- William Shakespeare, *The Tempest*

The Button

I get the text from Mike. I'm at such a low moment that I nearly cry with relief when I hear it bleep. Rummaging through the fallen debris, I scramble around the cabin to find the pager. When I pry it open and read Mike's message, the blood drains from my face.

"BATTEN DOWN THE HATCHES. THE WORST IS COMING, MATE."

No strategies. No plans. The message is a death knell. There's no way out.

How can it get any worse?

My mind falls into a kind of limbo. Nothing seems real. As my brain starts shutting down, my Royal Marine training kicks in. I don't need to think. I know what to do. Every single thing I do in these moments comes straight out of the *Commando Survival Training* book. Survival tactics have been drilled into me so hard and for so long that they're second nature. All I know is that my best chance for survival is to get it exactly right. I don't think at all.

In the carnage of the cabin, with my kit scattered all over, I struggle into my GUL thermals, dry suit, and life jacket. My hands shake as I fill a bag with anything I can find to help me survive if, as I fear, I have to abandon *Little Murka*. I push a fistful of flares into the grab bag and stare at the EPIRB. Maybe I'm not in "imminent danger" of dying, but this is a very dangerous situation. If the worst is to come, all I can do is prepare. I crouch down in the cabin, poised for action, wondering what's going to happen next.

I don't have to wait long.

The sea settles it. Grabbing *Little Murka* by force, she flips us over. And we roll. As she goes under, I fall hard against the cabin roof. I'm ready to keep rolling, as we bob back upright, but there's an eerie pause, which is long enough for me to glance out the hatch. We're completely underwater. Air bubbles glug up to the surface, but we're not coming back up. Something's wrong. It's probably 10 seconds, but it feels like 10 years.

Then *Little Murka* shakes it off. With a sudden splash, we're right-side up again, bobbing on the water, back to normal. I'm spooked. She's supposed to be self-righting. The designer put 80kg in the keel to make sure she'd flip back up, but she didn't as quickly as she should have. I'm confused.

There's no time to think before the next wave hits. We go over again. With no sea anchor to hold us into the gale, the wind has free rein and is now toying with us. It can just keep driving us up the side of the waves to then drop us off the top to tumble back down the face over and over and over until we can take no more. I regain my breath, but *Little Murka* is punched hard by a wave, sending us over again. Every moment we're upside down, there's a greater risk of water seeping in. If that happens, it will have a negative impact on the boat's ability to self-right. I have to do something while I have the chance. Standing inside the roof, I ram my pummelled body against the walls as hard as I can, like a bull in a pen, hoping it will nudge her to roll back up again. It does get her rocking, but it's not enough. Just before I panic, she comes back up. I feel a kind of desperate glee—I even laugh—but my nerves are shattered. I kneel upright, shaken.

I try to talk myself down. "No worries, Dom. We're all right. Just bail the water out and then…"

The very next wave flips us over. This time, it feels cruel like a schoolyard bully shoving a screaming kid's face back under the water again. On the third roll, we stay under for even longer. *What if we don't come back up?*

Instinctively, I reach for the EPIRB. Once activated, it will transmit a distress signal to be picked up by satellites that will triangulate my position to within 100 metres anywhere in the world. The nearest Search and Rescue unit will immediately receive the distress signal.

But I don't hit the EPIRB. According to the Maritime Codes of Practice, I'm not technically supposed to activate the EPIRB until I'm in "grave and imminent danger of bodily harm or death." I know perfectly well that 70% of fatalities on the water occur when a seaman falls overboard or his boat capsizes. We've just capsized for the third time. There's no question I should activate the EPIRB; I'm upside down. Yet, as I kneel on the ceiling of the cabin, being swallowed alive by the waves, I start having a dilemma.

I'm a marine. I can't hit the EPIRB. This isn't imminent danger. I can breathe, can't I? Before I can start arguing with myself, *Little Murka* rights herself again.

Immediately, the cabin starts flooding. With every roll, things are getting worse. I struggle to keep the electrical kit dry, on the off chance that I'm alive to use it later, but even the marine inside me has to admit that things are looking grim. I'm in a nightmare.

Dom, you are now in distress. Hit the fucking button.

I resist.

Through the window, the sky is black. It's probably daylight by now, but the suffocating clouds are fierce and menacing, a prelude to something even worse. Mike was right. There's no way out of this. Looks like my epitaph will read "Dom Mee, Lost at Sea."

It's always the risk, I suppose. It's some consolation that I'm in good company. Knowing I've never experienced such conditions cheers me up a little. At least I know I've gone down fighting the worst of them.

Hit the fucking button!

Even if I do set off the EPIRB now, no ship can reach me in 70kn winds. They can send a plane to track my location, but a pilot can do nothing at all for me. He can watch me die.

I believe in God, but I don't believe God can help those who don't show their faith through their actions, and I'm not talking about going to church on summer Sunday mornings. If prayers are to protect me, I'll have to do everything humanly possible to make a miracle happen. The boat rolls again for the fifth time. This time, we stay inverted. I desperately try to use my weight to right her. After about two minutes, she comes up slowly, but on each roll, she is slower to recover. There is something very wrong. The cabin is now awash with sea water, and I pick up the EPIRB. I stare at the sliding switch.

Hit the fucking button!

This would mean defeat after fighting so hard on this voyage. I've given it everything I have. There also comes the huge responsibility that sliding this switch will send someone else into this gale, risking their life to get me.

What if they die?

The reality is that if I don't hit the switch, I'll die.

Hit the fucking button!

I hit the switch, and the strobe light illuminates the cabin. It's a sorry sight. I'm in distress.

I've failed.

This is now uncharted territory. I know one thing for sure: no ship will be anywhere near me in this weather; shipmasters would have given this storm a wide berth.

I feel the boat get sucked up by a wave, and we are rolled again. As I stand on the ceiling of the boat, my painful shoulder is, once again, being rammed against the bulkhead. I'm in agony. After five minutes, with water rushing in through the solar vent, it's clear that she's not coming up again. The more the water inundates *Little Murka*, the less chance that she will right. I'm now faced with the ultimate dilemma.

This is the moment I've tried to put to the back of my mind; it's more frightening than anything else I've yet encountered. I'll have to leave the cabin of carnage to face the raging torrent above. I now understand why many captains in these circumstances go down with their ships: it's a choice between a quick death beneath the waves and a slow, terrifying death on the surface.

Little Murka was designed to survive and not sink due to the sealed compartments in her hull. My only hope is to try to stay on the keel.

The water in the cabin is rising slowly. I have to wait for the pressure to equalise before opening the hatch to swim to the nightmare that awaits on the surface. Before I turn the handle, I fumble through the debris sloshing around in the cabin. There is a miniature of Glenfiddich single malt whisky I've been saving for my 35th birthday. It seems wiser not to wait; I may die at 34. I take a swig, wish myself luck, and then down the rest with a toast to *Little Murka*: "Thanks, sweetheart. Stick by me if you can."

The water rushes in like a boot to the head. Half the air is knocked out of me as I fall back. I'm submerged. An arm snakes around my waist as I pull myself back through the hatch, and I try to shake off the sensation as a symptom of panic. But it isn't an illusion. Something, or someone, is holding me. Another arm latches on to my leg, and I suppress the urge to scream out every drop of oxygen in my lungs; I need the energy. Panic closes in, trapping me in a space as claustrophobic as the tiny cabin.

I tear at the arm around my waist, imagining it is some sea demon intent on dragging me to the ocean's bed. My lungs are blistering and my hands numb before a flashgun explodes behind my eyes as my head slams into *Little Murka*'s deck. The knock returns my senses: this isn't a tentacled demon; I'm snared in the kite lines. The loop round my waist slips free as I twist, but the heavy-duty line on my boot is holding me like a noose. I scramble at it with the toes of my other foot, but it's hopeless. I have no choice but to double over and free it with my hands. I breach the surface and take seven or eight breaths of water and air. The blurred sky is growing light, skyscraper waves surging upwards to meet it. The wind is too strong for me to breathe, and I'm gagged as it rams into my face. I free myself and surface immediately, hooking my harness to the deck gear.

Stay with the boat.

I clamber onto the harness I've managed to attach to myself. I heave myself onto the hull, spread my arms and legs in a starfish shape, and press my head to the yellow body like a newborn hugging its mother.

Stay with the boat. The mantra swills around my head.

The conditions are terrifying; the massive waves are taunting me, and the ear-puncturing winds are off the scale. I immediately hit my second panic button the personal locator beacon. This beacon is on the aircraft frequency transmitting on 121 MHz. It transmits a siren tone. I hit this beacon to highlight to the Coast Guard how bad my situation is. In these conditions, I need all the help I can get; yet, I would be near impossible to spot in a visual search.

It is cold. In desperation, I pull a red flare from my grab bag and fire it into the air. The wind grabs the rocket flare and blows it horizontal into the sea. If it wasn't so desperate, it would be funny.

The very poor visibility further hampers the little chance of being seen. My despair turns to anger. I've fought like a warrior these past days, the Atlantic giving me no quarter.

I kneel up and spit into the ocean. "Fuck you, you fucking bitch! You're not taking me!"

My survival brain kicks in, and I console myself: "OK, Dom, you've made your point. Conserve your energy."

The wind cuts into my face, feeling like shards of glass. I try to shelter my head behind the keel, but I'm repeatedly being washed overboard by these huge, incessant waves. I'm using precious energy to clamber back on the tiny keel that grows every time I fall in the freezing water. I'm getting weaker while the wind tries to suck every bit of heat from my body. The problem is that I know exactly what is happening. I'm trained to survive in any environment as a commando—not only to survive but also to fight a much larger enemy. For 15 years, this was my purpose. After four hours on the hull, I'm fighting my biggest foe.

My body is showing the early signs of hypothermia. In such a situation, a positive mental attitude can make a big difference. I start to calculate both a helicopter's and a ship's rescue time in these conditions. It's clear that a helicopter isn't coming, but I theorise to keep the grey matter alive. My calculations for a ship to arrive are correct, even though they don't give me the answer I want. I need to prepare for at least a 30-hour wait.

The battering continues, and the storm is not calming; if anything, it's getting worse. I'm starting to fade. If I sleep, I may not wake up. Some say it's not a bad way to go—just drift off and expire. I shake off the darkness and try to focus, but deep down, I know I'm not going to survive 30 hours in this weather. I'm knocked back into the sea.

I struggle back onto the hull, totally exhausted. My body is starting to malfunction. I see my destiny. A truly gigantic wave bears down on the boat. It sucks us up to face its peak, and I feel I can touch the sky, before it breaks and throws me away. I drop 60ft, and the wave is going to break on top of us. I let go. It's my time. I feel peace. I don't feel anything as I make impact with the ocean. The mega wave crashes down on top of me, pushing me further below the waves to the depths below.

I am done.

> "'Never get out of the boat.' Absolutely goddamn right! Unless you were goin' all the way… Kurtz got off the boat. He split from the whole fuckin' program."
>
> — *Apocalypse Now*

***

The duty watch keeper at the UK Coastguard Agency in Falmouth, England receives a call from the Joint Rescue Coordination Centre (JRCC) in Halifax, Nova Scotia, Canada. They have an EPIRB activation in their area of responsibility from a beacon registered to Falmouth. The duty watch keeper in Falmouth pulls up the details, along with the registered emergency contact person.

He calls Titch. "Hi, is this Adrian Wibrew?"

"Yes, speaking."

"Adrian, I'm the duty watch keeper at Falmouth Coast Guard. We are currently responding to a distress call from *Little Murka* in the north Atlantic. When did you last have contact with vessel?"

"We heard by email about thirty hours ago, but there was a big storm heading his way."

"OK, Adrian, thank you. We'll keep you updated."

Titch feels sick and has to sit down. It's the call he never wanted to receive and the one he's had nightmares about since waving Dom goodbye from St John's.

Falmouth confirms to the JRCC that the distress is genuine, that they are in contact with a dedicated person ashore, and that one crew member is on board the vessel. The JRCC issues a Maritime Assistance Request for any ships in the area to help with the rescue.

The JRCC staff are responsible for the distribution of essential information and arranging the dispatch of surface and air assets to respond to a rescue. A C130 Hercules aircraft, flight *Rescue 313*, has been scrambled to try to locate *Little Murka*.

Titch receives the call from the JRCC watch keeper. "Have you found the boat?" blurts out Titch in panic.

"No, sir. We are out there trying to locate the boat. We need to know what communication equipment he has on board."

"Not much. The phones went down days ago. His Mini-C may be working."

Titch silently makes a cup of tea and contemplates phoning Ang. He tries to think about how best he should word it: "Dom, as far as we know, is still alive. Keep positive."

But the final words from the watch keeper hang in his thoughts: "The conditions for rescue are far from ideal. He's in a massive storm with a mountainous swell. We'll try our best."

Titch ponders whether the watch keeper is trying to prepare him for the worst.

In the North Atlantic, *Berg Nord* is en route from Seven Islands, Canada and is carrying iron ore to Rotterdam. It is located on the edge of the storm system. At 305m long, she is one of the largest bulk carriers in the world and the biggest ship ever to enter the Arctic Circle. The Indian Captain, Ainsley Athaide, receives the request for assistance from the JRCC. As a seasoned mariner, he knows that in these conditions, it would be difficult for any vessel with a length of under 30m to survive. He contacts his company to ask permission to respond.

World shipping is a well-oiled machine. The *Berg Nord* will have barges waiting in Rotterdam to transport the iron ore to the steel mills in Germany. It is key that he stay as close to schedule as possible when crossing the world's oceans. Ships are not required by law to respond to a distress at sea. He could ignore the request, and that would be that; many ships do. Captain Athaide doesn't and immediately sets course for *Little Murka*'s last known position. The Coast Guard ship *CCGS Cygnus* is dispatched from St John's to head to *Little Murka*'s position. Captain Brian Penney informs the JRCC that he has deployed with his 20 crew members. The *CCGS Cygnus* is 63m overall and equipped with an MBB 105 helicopter and heavy-weather recovery RIB. She is a high-endurance, all-weather, offshore, ice-strengthened, multiple-role patrol vessel. If she can't save Dom, there is little chance anyone else can.

Titch picks up the phone. "Hi, Ang, it's T. I have some bad news."

Ang sits down and prepares.

"Dom's activated his EPIRB. I've spoken to the Canadian Coast Guard. They're going to get him."

"Have they seen him? What happened?" Ang replies, stunned.

"Put the kettle on. Sandy and I will pop over." Titch tries to sound reassuring.

En route, Titch rings Peter Beardow at 7E. "Peter, it's Titch"

"Yeah, OK, OK. I'm working on a solution for Dom's Mini-C as we speak, but I need a couple more hours."

Titch butts in. "Peter, Dom's hit the EPIRB."

"Oh."

"The JRCC is trying to get a better fix on his position, as the sea is huge. Can you get anything from the Mini-C remotely?"

"I'll get back you." Peter is on the case.

C130 Flight Rescue 313, commanded by Jean-Pierre Lafleur, arrives in the search area. After several sweeps, the crew has no visual, and the radar picks up no targets.

Jean calls into the JRCC, "No sign of the vessel; the casualty could be in the water."

Titch's phone rings. "Hello, Adrian. JRCC here. Does Dom have any other locator beacons with him?"

"Only the ones he's activated. What's happening?"

"Still ongoing. We haven't located him yet, but we will let you know."

Jean in the cockpit looks at his copilot. "Let's switch to infrared and sweep again."

They give each other a knowing look. This doesn't look good.

"Though an army encamp against me, my heart does not fear;
Though war be waged against me, even then do I trust."

- Psalm 27:3

The Miracle

I close my eyes. Lifeless under the waves, there is no noise. I feel like I'm suspended in my mother's womb. I have no life-flashing moments—just total calm. It feels wonderful. I submit to the end of my world.

I feel a sharp tug around my waist. In my delirium, I think it's an angel taking me away. I surface. I exhale, sputtering, and take a breath of life.

How am I alive?

My eyes slowly open to the harsh realities of being alive—the deafening wind still roars, and the sea continues to punch me in the face; yet, I feel no pain. I am numb.

I see something impossible. *Little Murka* is the right way up. I don't know how I do it or where it comes from, but my primordial survival instinct transforms me from a near-lifeless corpse to a wild man who is hell bent on living.

Go, go, go! Move, move, move!

I'm hard targeting, ready to storm a machine gun nest. I've only one more shot. I've been given a second chance at life. I have only three things to do:

Try to stop the boat capsizing.

Bail the boat of water so I can get inside.

Live.

If I can get the first two right, the odds of completing the third improve.

I swim towards *Little Murka*, my only place of refuge in the world right now. I climb on board and make a quick assessment. While clinging to the hull, I'd noticed that my water containers on either side of the hull had come loose, which was probably the main reason *Little Murka* didn't self-right. I grab my Leatherman from inside the cabin door. I struggle with dexterity, as my hands are numb. I immediately cut the containers off and throw them overboard.

Think, think stability.

Bucket.

I have no bucket, but I have a kite. I dive into the cabin's bow store, where I keep the kites, and I grab a roll of Dyneema line along with all the kites. First, I tie a line to the bow and turn the 5m kite into an improvised parachute anchor. I lower it into the sea and, submerging it slowly, pull the line to get it fully underwater. I ease the line out, and it goes tight. It's working. The bow, however, is not coming around to point into the wind. The kite isn't big enough. I repeat the process with the 10m kite, which should make all the difference. I attach the kite to the new roll of Dyneema line and let the roll do the work. Halfway through the roll, I discover that the bastard who sold it to me cut the line halfway. The kite is lost and descends into the abyss. *OK, focus.*

I grab anything with any weight, tie it to 30m of line, and throw it over the side. Every rope on board is used. I do all this urgently before a big wave capsizes us again. I then focus my energy on the next task—to bail the water out of the cabin.

Shit. I've nothing to bail out with. Think, Dom, think!

All I have to bail with is my grab bag. It seems an impossible task. For every bagful of water going out, in comes more spray from a wave or a gust of iron-hard raindrops. I know if I can bail out the cabin, I might have a hope of riding out the storm, and someone might find me alive. Bailing keeps the blood flowing, but I can't feel my hands or feet. It's impossible to warm saturated skin, and I'm a million miles away from being dry.

I start to think of the people who make life worth living: Ang, my family, my mates, and the team who've spent 18 months planning this record attempt with me. With all my training, it's simply love that gives me strength in these dark hours.

As I bail from the deck, I keep an eye on the waves. I'm so scared of going over again; there's too much water in the boat, and she'll stay over. I won't last long in this. I cannot believe what surrounds me. The storm has got worse, and everything takes on a deeper, darker shade of ominous. I pray it will soon abate. I'm bailing like a lunatic. I hear the recognisable roar of a big wave charging towards us. I dive in the cabin and lock the hatch. *Little Murka* lurches heavily on her side as the sheer tonnage explodes into us.

No, please, no.

She comes back up.

Bail, bail, bail. It's a huge task, but I'm starting to see the fruits of my labour as the cabin water is slowly decreasing. I bail harder. After two hours and four big waves, most of the water is out. I crawl inside the cabin. To be out of the smothering wind is heaven.

My food is stored in sealable bags, and I have fresh water in the bow compartment. I grab my video camera and send a farewell message just in case things don't work out. I want to leave them with something of my final moments. It's a visual last letter, a remote goodbye, and an extremely unpleasant thing to do.

The lines to my makeshift sea anchor seem to be holding—but only just. We list over slowly with every wave. I pray we don't go over again. I'd emptied the grab bag in a compartment free of water before I'd started bailing. I check for any item of use in the hours ahead. It's then that I find 20 cigarettes that I'd put in the grab bag. I can't believe it. I'd obviously done it in St. John's as a "just in case." There are five waterproof matches taped to the pack. I desperately try to light one but with no luck. Waterproof matches are always hit and miss, but my last match springs to life. I take a drag and feel the warm smoke enter my body. I've been craving a smoke for the last two weeks. I chain smoke the whole pack. My head is buzzing from the nicotine overload, and I can feel my core body temperature rising. There flickers a sliver of hope.

Out of nowhere, we are hit by a massive wave.

Shit, shit, shit.

I fall onto the roof and then roll down the side of the cabin. I'm back in the *Little Murka* washing machine. She rights herself straight away. It was clearly the water containers that had prevented previous righting. The deck is now clear of all obstructions. I sit motionless in shock. *She's come back up*, I tell myself. *This is good.*

What isn't good is the storm outside. It's just horrendous; the sea state is off the scale. I am still far from out of the woods. I just pray the Hail Mary like a mantra nonstop.

I think I hear a plane. I look out. Nothing. I keep checking the EPIRB to make sure it's working. A comforting flashing green/red light tells me it's fine. Doubts claw at my mind as I sit here. I remain focused, but I'm utterly terrified. We go over another six times, but the indefatigable *Little Murka* comes back up, thank God. The only doubt is whether the boat will hold together in this raging tempest. She's been tossed around like a matchstick for longer than I care to remember. I shudder to think what it's doing on the Grand Banks. It's horrific here. We are being rolled around once every hour.

I open one of my ration bags. I haven't eaten now for around 15 hours. I know I've got to eat and to drink fresh water to keep my strength up. I try a chocolate bar and throw it back up. I try again and vomit again. I've got to eat. The situation is so desperate and terrifying that it's hard to keep anything down. The stress is unbearable; I am locked into a storm with the power of a nuclear missile. Outside, over the blast of the ocean, I hear an answering sound that isn't the storm. It's a throbbing noise that makes the boat vibrate... a mechanical noise... an engine. I fling open the hatch, pull myself half on deck and start waving my arms wildly. For a few seconds, I can't see anything, and then a Hercules aircraft roars overhead so low that the wave crests are almost licking its propellers. I briefly smell the fumes of the aviation fuel, and my heart lifts. It reminds me of those halcyon days parachuting from a Hercules tailgate when in the Royal Marines.

I grab one of my handheld flares and pull the pin. ALIVE.

The heavy red smoke covers my face before streaming out across the ocean. I watch the plane circle back around slowly. The pilot tips his wings and flashes his landing lights. They kick out a life raft, but it blows miles from me, tumbling away in the high winds like a gymnast across the ocean. It's a shame; I could have really used it. Not by getting in it, as I was safer in *Little Murka*, but I could've used it for stability. If I'd used my knife to slash the air out of the life raft and sank it below the surface, it would have made a massive sea anchor and helped me to ride out the storm.

The Hercules comes around for another pass. I watch two bags fall from the tailgate on a 50m line. I manage to grab the line, but I don't open the bags; they're quite heavy. I don't need food and water, so I tie the bags off the bow and stern to give me stability. It works pretty well. The sea is still pumping, but I manage to eat a small pack of nuts and drink some fresh water. I'm comforted, as by now, Ang and the family will know I'm alive. They must have all been at their wits' end.

I'm brutally reminded of my extremely precarious situation as I'm hit again by a gigantic wave. When I dare to open the hatch to check on the plane and see if any vessels have arrived, I see the sea in all its glorious anger. I start to think how I'm going to get on board another ship in these conditions. I make a promise to myself that if it involves jumping off *Little Murka* to try to get to a cargo net hung down the side of a ship, I'm not going to try it, especially at night. This option in these conditions and my fairly weakened state would mean certain death. If I'm washed away in these waves, I'll never be seen again.

As I'm pondering these nightmare scenarios, a massive wave picks up the boat. I dive inside the cabin just before the boat starts to go over. While upside down, I lunge at the handle to secure the hatch as sea water pours in. I secure one side, but we are over again. We are rolling down the face of this gigantic wall of water. I bang my head; we are still rolling. The cooker dislodges itself and flies off, hitting me hard in the ribs, and I'm defenceless against the cabin debris that pummels me from all angles. After the sixth roll, we hit the bottom. The worst is to come, as the aftershock of the wave breaks on top of us. A thousand white stallions stampede down on us. I crawl into a ball as we are violently pushed along by thousands of tons of water. I close my eyes. We go over again as the wave comes through. The cabin is waterlogged, but it could have been much worse. I grab the cooker and throw it into the raging torrent.

"Hail Mary, full of grace, the Lord is with thee."

The plane circles reassuringly, dropping carpets of flares so they can keep a fix on me. It's eerie to see the flares burn on the surface in between the waves. It looks more like it should be in the movie *Apocalypse Now*. In my fragile state, it's like a weird dream. It's starting to get dark.

> "I watch a snail crawl along the edge of a straight razor. That's my dream, that's my nightmare. Crawling, slithering, along the edge of a straight razor... and surviving."
>
> - Colonel Kurtz, *Apocalypse Now*

***

Titch and Peter in the UK are frantically trying to send satellite pager messages to Dom to inform him that the search aircraft is overhead.

Titch calls Ang. "They've found *Little Murka*."

"What about Dom?"

"Nothing yet. He probably hasn't heard the plane," he says lamely.

Silence.

Titch receives another call from the JRCC. They play a recording from Captain Jean saying "We have a visual on deck. He fired a hand flare; he's alive."

Titch shares the good news with everyone. Titch and Ang work on a press release for the general public and our sponsors. The *Berg Nord* is getting nearer to *Little Murka's* last reported position. The *Cygnus* is now in the storm, and they have to slow right down due to the terrible conditions. It looks like, at best, they will reach the search area the following morning. Rescue Flight 131 calls JRCC Halifax to inform them of their low fuel and requests clearance to fly back to base. Halifax has already dispatched Rescue Flight 116 to continue the over watch.

Angels and the Unpaid Ferryman

The plane flying overhead flashes its landing lights in Morse code. I wish I'd spent more time learning the code, and I don't have a Morse table guide. The plane then flies off into the distance. I'm alone again, and the separation hurts more than ever, like leaving a loved one. Just as I return solemnly to the cabin, I hear another plane fly overhead. I'm humbled that they've sent another plane. All this help for just me. A tear stings my eye. It's very important not to let my guard down. A plane can't do much for me. I have to keep focused. I've no idea when help will arrive, but it should be in around six hours, based on my mental calculations when on the hull. The sea state is still huge, but the wind has eased a little. I'm guessing it's down to 40kn; my wind meter disappeared during one of the many capsizes. My method of guesstimating the wind speed is that it is strong but not trying to rip off my head as it was four hours ago.

Incredibly, I see Peter flying along the waves. My heart lifts, and then I realise that it might not be Peter. In all the stress, I haven't thought about my travelling companion. Guilt creeps in.

The plane flies a little lower, flashing Morse code, but I still can't work it out. They are trying to tell me something. I look around and scan what I can of the horizon in this swell. I see lights... a ship. I get my binoculars and try to look at the large, dark silhouette. I make out the red port light. Her stern is pointing into the waves. The sea is still wild. I'm still in mortal danger even so close to another vessel.

I remember doing my Coastal Skipper course with Royal Marines instructor Steve Higgs 10 years before. He took us all out off Plymouth Sound in a force 8 to conduct man-overboard drills using a bucket with a strobe light attached. It taught me a very valuable lesson—never leave the boat. It also demonstrated how difficult it is to spot someone in the water. On board *Little Murka*, if I stand up, my head is roughly around 7ft above the water. The seas around me are around 50ft.

The massive, dark ship is getting closer. The searchlight switches on and looks like a Martian laser beam scanning the sea. I know that the seaman behind the searchlight will do his level best to find me. As anyone who travels the sea knows, one day it could be any of us in the water. The searchlight is located around 100ft up on the bridge wings, yet it seems to point anywhere but on me. The light eventually swings right on me. I fire off my handheld flare. The sea around me turns red from the burning torch, and it looks like the blood from a mass murder. The searchlight moves away. I am frustratingly invisible. I can see that Rescue Flight 116 is signalling in Morse code to the ship and presumably talking to them on VHF. The light again searches everywhere I am not. I'm ready with a small handheld rocket flare and fire it just as the light swivels in my direction, but the flare is blown away by the evil wind. The searchlight is distracted by the flare and starts searching in another area.

The ship has been trying to locate me for around two hours, and permanently exposed to the elements, I'm getting dangerously cold. I see the ship pulling away. The captain is probably worried about running me over. I know instantly that he's going to wait for first light before attempting again. He's a good captain. It's a cautionary note to all sailors: I've been standing on the deck of a bright yellow boat, waving a handheld flare, and the ship hasn't seen me in over two hours of meticulous searching. I withdraw to the cabin to recuperate and warm up. I must remain focused. It may not be possible to get on the ship because of the weather. It might be a long wait; I need to be strong. I settle into a kind of sleep for about two hours. I stick my head out of the cabin to check on things. The ship's presence consoles me, and the rescue plane is still on station.

God bless them all.

The swell has calmed considerably in the last few hours, but I don't rest on my laurels; on this voyage, anything can happen. Through the night and past dawn, I watch the shadows of the ship and the plane, waiting for the seas to quell enough for me to escape. A full 24 hours have passed since I struggled out of the flooded cabin. The new day starts to reveal itself. I can make out more details of the ship that has come to my assistance. I grab my binoculars and scan the ship, searching to see what kind of crane she has. I wonder if she will be able to lift *Little Murka* on board. The boat has taken such a beating, but she's never failed me; the thought of abandoning her is just not cricket. I'm so attached to her, as well as to Peter, who is back in in his normal position behind the boat. It's difficult to comprehend.

As I scan the ship, I'm surprised by an orange and white Coast Guard ship that appears out of nowhere. The captain and 20 crew of the *Cygnus* have sailed through the night to save me. The *Cygnus* stands off 100m and starts to launch the RIB. Peter takes to the air. That's the last I see of him.

Goodbye, dear friend. I will meet you again in my dreams.

"It was morning, and the new sun sparkled gold across the ripples of a gentle sea."

- Jonathan Livingston Seagull

The conditions have calmed so much. Six hours ago, it would have been impossible to launch a RIB. I point at all my lines in the water so they don't snag their propeller, and they come around on the safe side to rescue me.

The coxswain is professional and talks in an urgent tone. "Get your stuff. We're going now. We have another weather system coming in."

I immediately ask if they can crane *Little Murka* on board, and the coxswain asks the captain over the radio.

"OK, we'll put her on a tow, but if she comes off, that's it," he states officially.

"Thanks, and thanks for coming," I reply humbly.

It all happens so quickly. For some reason, I leave all my equipment on board; I'm not thinking straight. The first thing I want to do is let Ang and the family know I'm safe.

They tie *Little Murka* behind the *Cygnus* and then winch the RIB and me on board. First things first, in the tradition of the sea, I introduce myself to the captain and thank him. I also apologise for all the fuss I've caused. I ask permission to use the VHF to thank Captain Athaide of the *Berg Nord*, who has valiantly tried to help me. Finally, I ask if I can use the phone to call my wife.

I speak to Ang. She is massively relieved to hear my voice, as I am to hear hers; it's been a very close call. I ask her to let Mum, Dad and Sian know that I love them. Captain Brian Penney is a great guy and a wise captain who has seen more than his fair share of mountainous seas and tragedy in his job. With a lifetime of saving others, instead of hardening him, he is a man with a great sense of humanity, and the warmth of his spirit touches me. I explain what happened. I feel embarrassed that I've had to be rescued; a commando hates nothing more than failing a mission.

He must sense my regret. "There's some bacon on the grill, if you're up to it," Captain says with a big smile.

A bacon sandwich after 40 days on dehydrated food? Now there's a thought. I haven't eaten much in the last 24 hours, and I'm dog-tired, but I reckon I could squeeze in a bacon butty.

I'm worried about how the crew of the *Cygnus* will judge me. Will they think me a damn fool, without knowing how hard I tried in those 40 days in hell? I nervously go below to the galley. On the way, I meet a few of the crew, who all shake my hand and welcome me on board. I'm relieved.

I arrive at the hot plate and am greeted by the chef, who is bearing a big smile. "Now, there's a man who could use some breakfast."

I sit down. Most of the crew has already eaten, so I eat alone. I'm safe. It feels really weird; I almost can't believe it's all over. The ordeal has finally ended. It's been horrendous.

The crew gives me a set of overalls and flip-flops, as I have no clothes. I ask a passing crew member if he has a cigarette.

"Give me a minute," he says and returns with another crew member, who is holding a carton of 200. "Have these, young fella. I've plenty, and I reckon you need a smoke after what you've just been through."

I go to the poop deck at the rear of the ship. I thought the last cigarette I smoked might have been my last. Like a concerned father, I look at *Little Murka* on the tow. I really hope she'll make it back.

The captain has organised a berth in the sickbay. I'm barely awake when I get to my bed, but first, I have one thing to do. I write down what's happened while it's fresh in my mind. I fall asleep with the pen in my hand. I sleep for eight hours.

I look through the cabin window as daylight wakes me; the wind is back up. This ocean is just a nonstop wind machine. I head down to the poop deck for a cigarette and check on *Little Murka*. This becomes an hourly ritual, as I want to protect her. She's battled through the worst that this ocean can throw at her, and she's still fighting. She's one hell of a boat.

The wind is up to 20kn+. I talk to one of the crew, who also shares my filthy habit. We exchange pleasantries as one does. I ask him what he knew of my situation when they received my distress signal.

"I'll be frank with you. The captain prepared us to pick up a body. We've had a bad run over the last few months."

I recount my ordeal and how, when I thought it was over, I was saved by the big wave. "My God, you were lucky. We normally put the bodies in there." He points to a compartment on the poop deck.

I think of how close I was to lying in there, wrapped in a body bag. It sends a shiver down my spine.

"The ship is different when we intern a body. Everyone is on edge. We know we have to get them home to their families, but it's a sad thing to do. None of us like it. We do this to save lives." We've been chain-smoking during the conversation. "I'll tell you one thing: the mood on the ship lifted when we saw you alive."

I head for my cabin to try to sleep. It's not easy after my ordeal.

I wake the next morning on my 35th birthday, one that I nearly didn't reach. I'm asked to the bridge to see the captain.

"Happy Birthday, Dom. We have some messages from home."

I thank the kind captain and read the good wishes from friends and family. It's a strange birthday, but I couldn't have wished to be in better company. They are a great bunch of guys. At lunch, the crew makes me a birthday cake and all sing "Happy Birthday." *Little Murka* is still on the tow, and everyone is keeping a close eye on her; they, too, are feeling attached to my little girl.

"I thought she'd be off the tow in a couple hours," commented one of the deckhands. "She rides well in the water for such a small craft."

The captain calls me to the bridge with sad news: *Little Murka* has come off the tow. He's bringing the ship around to see what can be done. I immediately go to the sickbay, put on my dry suit, and return to the bridge. "Captain, I'll go over the side and reattach the tow." The captain looks at me gravely. "I don't want you going over the side. Let's see what we can do."

"I understand, Captain, but if you change your mind, I'll be waiting on the lower deck ready to go."

They try everything to get her back on but, alas, nothing can be done. I'm so tempted to go over the side, but I'm a military man, and after all the captain has done for me, it would be wrong to disobey him.

It's good to be alive, but I'm really sad to lose *Little Murka*. The Atlantic has taken its last swipe; *Little Murka* is back on the Grand Banks. I have to be philosophical and concede that if this was the price to pay for surviving, then that's the way it is. I hope someone, somewhere will find her. I'd prayed for a miracle to save my life, and that's what I'd got. The sea took everything else.

"We must free ourselves of the hope that the sea will ever rest. We must learn to sail in high winds."

- Aristotle Onassis

Back on the Foredeck

I receive a message from Titch. He's booked me back into Leeside Manor and informs me that Clinton Rogers from the BBC is bringing out some clothes and money. I became friends with Clinton after he covered all my expeditions over the years. He started as a 16-year-old journalist working for local newspapers, and he covered the Gulf War from the Middle East. He worked his way up into television and was now the senior correspondent for BBC Points West.

The *Cygnus* slowly approaches the entrance to St John's harbour. I don't know what to expect. I'm hoping that I can slip in as quietly as I slipped out. I see the flashing lights of cameras as the *Cygnus* throws her lines ashore. It's a fair cop; the cameramen are only doing their job. I'd worked with the media while promoting my expedition for sponsors, so it comes with the territory. I arrange to meet the crew for a beer in the town later that evening. I say a very fond farewell to Captain Brian; he and his crew really looked after me, and I'm genuinely moved by their kindness.

On the dock, I hold an impromptu press conference and link up with Clinton and Jess Rudkin from BBC Somerset Sound Radio. A warm welcome awaits me at Leeside Manor. I slip into the bath and allow the stresses of the previous weeks to slowly soak away. The phone rings constantly, but I need peace for half an hour.

I dry myself off and fully appreciate the simplicity of lying in hot water. I answer the phone and do another interview. What I really need is to have a drink and be alone for an hour with some Newfie screech. I have to hang around in St John's to wait for a replacement passport, so I may have more than a bottle.

I order a taxi from reception and walk aimlessly around the cemetery adjacent to Leeside Manor to smoke. A raven flies into a tree and squawks at me loudly. Another 20 or so join in.

Weird, I think to myself.

I approach the birds. None budge; they just all squawk at me. There must be a logical explanation, but it freaks me out. I ask Nicole in reception if they have a problem with ravens at the hotel.

"I've worked here eight years, and I can't ever recall seeing a raven."

This is way too weird for me. It's time to jump into a bottle of rum.

I meet the *Cygnus* crew, along with Jess and Clinton, and have a few drinks against the backdrop of quality folk music. It still seems like a dream; yet, I've felt uneasy since coming ashore, as if something is following me. It's hard to explain, but it's extremely unnerving.

I return to the UK via a stopover in Montreal, where I check my emails for the first time since reaching dry land. I have grim news from my old friend Roman Cioma. He's extra glad that I'm alive as he recently carried former colleague Matt Bacon into a C1-30 for his final journey home. A roadside bomb killed Matt on the 11th of September in Al Basrah, Iraq. It doesn't seem fair.

I need to see a priest. I feel the need to offer a confession; it's been a long time since I've done so. I go to Notre Dame Basilica, where I try to see a priest who will hear my confession. I'm turned away, as they are hosting a high-society wedding. I walk across town to St Patrick's Basilica and am told that the priest is not to be disturbed. I feel dejected. The fat priests in Montreal have it pretty good. Unless you're a pop star, you don't get a look-in. I arrive back in the UK with this strange negative energy still with me. It's very emotional to see Ang and Titch again, and tears flow freely.

On the drive back to Somerset, I gaze out into space. I don't know what to say; I've failed. I also know that we faced financial ruin. A TV bus is camped outside White Gables awaiting my return. I conduct a further round of interviews. It's not a big deal, and I know most of the journalists. Finally, we can close the door on the world and reflect on what's happened.

"Please don't look at the blog on our website; there are lots of negative comments," says Ang.

I've no time for keyboard warriors, as I know few would have the balls to say it to my face. It is, however, upsetting for my family to read.

Business isn't going well either. Titch is working in the office on a PR contract I set up before I left to try to keep the money coming in, but we haven't been paid. The book deal that I thought we were going to get has also fallen through.

"It isn't quite the ending we were looking for," says my publishing agent, with little concept of what I'd endured. I hang up the phone, seething.

Titch has to find another job. I can't keep him on, even though we've been together throughout our Marine careers and all my expeditions. It's a pretty sad time. Luckily, one of our sponsors, John Wrelton, gives him a job working in his estate agent business.

Ang and I continue to struggle financially. Within a couple of days of getting back, I go back to sea with Team Murka, who is training in the Solent for the upcoming yacht-racing world championships in Key West. I need to go back to sea. It's like getting back on the bike after a fall. I also need to be around people who understood the ocean and understand the reality of what I've been through. I also have a chance to meet Mike to tell him firsthand what happened out there. We cast off from Port Humble and head out for race practice. I coil the dock lines on the foredeck and look at my bowman, Finley.

"Good to have my mast man back."

"Aye! It's good to be back too, shipmate," I reply before getting the foredeck ready for action.

"What can we gain by sailing to the moon if we are not able to cross the abyss that separates us from ourselves? This is the most important of all voyages of discovery, and without it, all the rest are not only useless, but disastrous."

- Thomas Merton

Return of the Prodigal Daughter

It's not how a man fails; it's how he gets back up, fists clenched and ready to take on life with vigour.

I'd already announced that I was going to try to break the Atlantic rowing record from the Canaries to the Caribbean before I'd embarked on Kite Quest 200. With my hair still wet from the North Atlantic, the quest for sponsorship continues for my next crossing. There's a record to break.

As I potter about my workshop, this negative energy I've had since St John's is getting worse, and it's really spooking me; I can't take it anymore. I immediately jump in the car and head to the local church, St Georges. The priest is on the steps as if he's waiting for me.

"I need you to hear my confession."

"That's what I'm here for. Come with me, my son."

He gets 10 years of my colourful life and sins. I walk out of the church, finally free of this negative energy. I can't explain it. Whatever it is, I'm glad to see the back of it.

August 2006, White Gables, Somerset

I'm busy making preparations for the weekend training session with my rowing team. The one thing Kite Quest 200 taught me was that time spent on the boat is time well spent. We are rowing from Exmouth to Salcombe, a small row of 40 miles, with a big night on the rum followed by a row back the following morning. I want to see how the team performs with a hangover. It's essential that I look out for any cracks in the guys.

My team assembles for the briefing. First in are Ed "Edwardo" James, Pete "Birdy" Bird, and, finally, Tom "T1000" Rendell. I'm waiting on a weather window from Mike. My phone rings. "Hello, this is the Prestwick Coast Guard. Is this Dom Mee?"

My confusion about their call is made all the more baffling when they ask if I have an expedition in the North Atlantic at the moment.

"We've no expeditions out at all. Why do you ask?"

"We've received an EPIRB activation registered to you."

I pause for a few seconds, trying to comprehend the information. "Is the beacon registered to a vessel called *Little Murka*?"

"Yes, that's correct."

My heart leaps. "Where is she?"

"The boat has been found by local fishermen in Malin Head, Ireland. I have a phone number if you want it."

I write down the number and sit down, not really believing what I've just heard.

Mike calls. "Hi, Domster. The weekend is looking like a 'no go'; there's a front moving through, and I wouldn't risk it."

"Thanks, Mike. Still giving me bad news forecasts? Some things don't change." We laugh. I tell him about the phone call from the Coast Guard. He can't believe it either: *Little Murka* turning up a year later.

I turn to the team. "Sorry, lads, this weekend's off due to a weather front, and I have to go to Malin Head, wherever that is."

I check my charts and find a little rocky outcrop at the most northern tip of Ireland. During World War II, the Irish government allowed the British government to site two radio direction finders on Malin Head. This top-secret operation was mentioned in *The Cranborne Report*. The RDF equipment was used to monitor U-boat and aerial activity in the North Atlantic. After the war, the site became a weather station for the Met Éireann and a Navtex transmitting station. I learnt to navigate with Navtex in the days before GPS. I stared at the number that the Coast Guard man gave me for Charlie O'Donnell, Shell Fish Co-operative.

"Hi, Charlie. I'm the owner of the boat you found. Please look after it. I'm on the way."

I also ring Clinton Rogers at the BBC and let him know. He's over the moon and asks me when I am going over to get her.

"Tomorrow."

Clinton laughs. He knows me too well. "I'm coming with you. This will be a great piece for the news."

I ring Titch, Louay, and Baz. All are intrigued by how it's even possible. I head to Bristol airport, where Baz has booked me a hire car. Clinton will meet me in Malin Head. I'd hoped that this day would come, but as the months passed by, I'd lost hope and assumed I'd never see her again.

In all the excitement, I've forgot one detail. I'm heading to Belfast, and the last time I was here, people were actively trying to kill me.

One of my closest friends, Si Parsons, was blown up on our tour of West Belfast in 1993. Thankfully, he survived. The ceasefire seems to be holding between all the paramilitary groups, and there's been a massive scaling down of military operations in the province. I'd never been back to Northern Ireland once I'd left the Marines; I'd had no real reason to go. The Ryan Air plane did its normal poor approach and bumped down the tarmac. The last time I'd landed here it was on an RAF Hercules C-130 out of Brize Norton with an equally bad landing. On my first tour in Belfast, 23 people were killed and 63 wounded in a spate of attacks and bombings on both sides of the divide in the first two weeks. At the time, Titch and I were part of Bravo Company, 40 Commando, stationed at New Barnsley Police Station. At the time, it was the most bombed police station in the Western world. These are my lasting memories of the place, and I'm about to drive across Belfast en route to Londonderry. I'm very attentive to the directions given to me by the friendly guy at the hire car desk. As I drive out of Belfast on the M22, I notice how different it is. It's strange in its normalcy: no checkpoints, no soldiers, and no armored RUC Hotspurs. I smile as I see a sign for Cookstown, another place where I served a tour. I'm driving down a road I've driven before. The previous time, I had a mate riding shotgun with an SA80 assault rifle, along with smoke grenades, and I had a Browning 9mm pistol at my side.

I arrived on the early flight, so I didn't have time for breakfast. The Northern Irish have many talents, but they do one thing amazingly well—breakfast. "The Ulster Fry" is hard to beat. I pull over into a small family-run roadside café, which is the best kind. My plate comes loaded with sausages, bacon, potato farls, eggs, and mushrooms, along with delicious soda bread. I'm now ready for the journey ahead to be reunited with my *Little Murka*.

I stop in Londonderry to buy a camera before heading over the border to the Republic of Ireland. Despite my family originating in Ireland, I've never visited the place. The roads narrow as I enter County Donegal and head north through the wild, windswept Irish coastline. It is breathtakingly beautiful. I'm staying at a hostel in Malin Head that Charlie has kindly arranged for me. I drop my bags off and head excitedly to the Shellfish Co-operative.

Charlie is a kind-hearted Irishman with wild hair and all the canniness for which the Irish are famous.

"She's still on the rocks where we found her. Well, we dragged her up a bit; it's not far." Charlie has recovered a fair bit of equipment from *Little Murka*. I have a quick look, but I'm more interested in seeing the boat. As I walk down the beach, many mixed emotions sweep over me. Then, I see her sitting there, battle-hardened in barnacles. I think of the sadness I felt when she drifted away on the Grand Banks. My *Little Murka* has come home, yet it's an unprecedented set of circumstances that has led to our reunion.

"We need to get her off the rocks; there's a storm due in. I'll organise some fellas. Let's meet at the beach after lunch."

The media in Ireland has picked up on the story, and Clinton has now arrived. I get back to the hostel, and the owner tells me that the phones have been ringing off the hook. I do the interviews, and Clinton shows me the video camera in its waterproof case. Most of the equipment has been destroyed through corrosion after a year at sea.

"I'll take it to Londonderry, as I have to edit your piece for tonight's news and see if the tape survived," says Clinton kindly.

I ring Uri Geller and tell him the story. He'd written *Powered by Uri* on the back of *Little Murka* when he'd named her, and he is delighted at the news.

I meet up with the guys Charlie has organised to help me lift the boat up the beach. It's a hot summer's day, and we have to lift *Little Murka* up a steep hill, past the rocks, and to a tractor that will do the rest of the pulling. We all take our shirts off. I look around at the other guys. Most have tattoos, one sporting *Tiocfaidh ár lá (Our Day Will Come)* at the base of the Irish Tricolour; it is an IRA slogan.

This could be interesting, I think.

It's obvious they can see my Royal Marines Commando tattoo shimmering on my sweaty right shoulder, so I make the first move. "Nice tattoo," I say jokingly to the lad with the tricolour. He returns a smile.

After the hard work of shifting the boat, I offer to buy the lads a pint down at the local pub. I meet the guys at Farren's Bar, and the beer quickly flows. I discover that Bernard McLauhlin, who is a cracking guy, found *Little Murka*.

"He thought it was a jet ski at first," Charlie jokes. "I told him not to mess about with the beacon, but he wouldn't listen."

Bernard had taken the EPIRB off its cradle and set it off.

Charlie cuts in, "I saw the lights go on. I said all hell's going to break loose now, you fool." They were a bit worried about opening the hatch at first. "We thought there may be a body in there," explains Bernard.

We talk about many things, including the troubles. I give my point of view as a soldier and return their perspective. I find the whole experience very positive, and despite sacrifices on both sides, it's clear that things are looking up in Northern Ireland.

Clinton returns and hands me the tape before joining us for a quick beer. "The footage is useable. It survived, and it's pretty powerful stuff. I'll only use a small piece."

I return with Jamie and Emily to collect *Little Murka* and transport her back to Somerset. Jamie gets her back into the workshop and fixes her up.

At home, I retire to my office, and the tape recovered from *Little Murka* is placed in my video player. I lock the door, open a bottle of Mount Gay rum, and sit comfortably. I press "play."

Restoration

"Being a survivor doesn't mean being strong—it's telling people when you need a meal or a ride, company, whatever. It's paying attention to heart wisdom, feelings, not living a role but having a unique, authentic life, having something to contribute, finding time to love and laugh. All these things are qualities of survivors."
- Bernie Siegel

January 2007, Puerto Tazacorte, Isla de la Palma, Atlantic Ocean

The big flurry to get ready is stressful. Everyone is running around to get last-minute spares for the boat and to sort out last-minute admin, including doing a naked photo shoot for *The Sun* newspaper. As Samantha Fox said, "You can't be taught to be brainy. You've either got it or you don't."

I know what side of the fence I'm on, so I get my kit off. I'll do pretty much anything to get some column inches for my sponsors.

The one thing I want is to bless the boat. Always in the back of my mind is *Little Murka* and me fighting the hurricanes; it's still hard to shake. I feel it's my personal responsibility for the team to return safely, and I promise as much to their families. It's the first time any of them has embarked on a challenge like this, and obviously, their families are concerned. I've the best team in ocean rowing by far. We've done hundreds of miles of training, even rowing from London to Paris. We've also taken part in the Great River Race, the biggest race in Europe, which takes place on the Thames in London. We took line honours, winning outright, and set a new record for the fastest ocean-rowing boat. The team is ready for the Atlantic. I can put my hand on my heart and say that this team is fully prepared.

I ring Rosie to organise a priest to attend. He arrives in his robes before blessing the boat, *Atlantic Quest*, with holy water, and he gives me the ladle to bless the crew. Pouring the water over their heads makes me well up. The weight of responsibility I have reflects to *Little*

Murka. I don't want these lads going through what I did 18 months ago. Some of our sponsors come over to see us off; Jim and Melanie Murrel from Inotec are great fun to be around.

I'm also aware that I've heaped pressure on the team to get this far. I've always pushed them to breaking point so I could see the cracks. I needed to see all their weaknesses before we set off onto the open ocean. After 18 months of solid preparation and brutal training, I need consolidation with the team because it's vital that we all work together crossing the ocean. I think long and hard about what I will say to my guys before we start the row in earnest. Mike's weather window means we need to embark tomorrow. We have our final meal—a last supper. My final speech at the table is simple: "Let's go to the beach."

The beaches at La Palma are grey from volcanic ash, a result of being a volcanic ocean island. The volcano rises almost 7km from the floor of the Atlantic Ocean. There's road access from sea level to the summit at 7,959ft, which is marked by an outcrop of rocks called Los Muchachos, translated in English as "The Lads." This is the site of the Roque de los Muchachos Observatory, one of the world's highest astronomical observatories. On my visit to the island a year ago, I ascended to the summit. It was a balmy 23 degrees at sea level, and by the time I reached the summit, I was in a snow blizzard.

I sit the lads down on the beach as the waves crash on shore.

"Everyone, dig a hole in the sand." The lads do as asked. "I know I've pushed you really hard, and we've had differences of opinion, but without each other, we won't cross the ocean. I want everyone to put all their negative feelings into the hole and cover it in. These things stay on this beach; they don't come on the ocean with us. Together, we will have to overcome many challenges ahead, and we will be stronger at the other end."

I'm confident that this makes a massive difference to the psychology of the team. Tomorrow, we will face a very powerful force. We need to be as one.

It's a special moment for the team; at last, we are going to do what we've all set out to do. Ninety percent of the work has been done. All that remains is the last 10%—the crossing itself. We set off with an escort of local boats and friends we've made in La Palma. The locals have been really supportive and helpful during our stay. We row out of the marina at Puerto Tazacorte and are joined by a colourful flotilla of around 20 yachts to bid us farewell. It's a striking contrast to the dark skies over *Little Murka* and me as we slipped out of St John's almost unseen. The yachts and friends soon drop behind the horizon, and we are on the deep ocean at last.

Ed and I do all the cooking and make all the water. Ed has learned to strip the water maker down blindfolded and solve its problems. It's critical to our success.

Birdy and Tom are in the forward cabin with Ed and I in the rear. I pair up to row with Birdy, and Ed will partner Tom. We may switch partners halfway, but I'll make the call at the right time.

For the first 10 days, we power along, well on course for the record. The weather is always a factor in ocean rowing, and going at the best time of year gives us the best chance for a quick crossing. There'll be no hurricanes this time. Mike calls to let me know we have a cold front from the Grand Banks to Cape Verde islands.

Damn the Grand Banks.

I'm thousands of miles south; yet, it still has me in its grip, reminding me not to forget. Unfortunately, this front puts us on the sea anchor for two days while strong headwinds try to push us back. The winds are dead north. We must try to head south. It's not ideal, but it's better than being on the sea anchor doing nothing. We have to get rowing. We've lost four days of westerly progress. We all know that to have a chance of breaking the record, we need to row every day, so losing four days is a cruel blow, but none of us are ready to give up yet. This is Team Quest.

The winds turn favourable. To have a chance, we have to row harder and faster than anyone before us. After 10 days, we manage to make up 24 hours of lost time. We enter a weather system of isolated thundery clouds that again slows us right down, but we dig deep, making up another 24 hours, despite it being hard rowing. We are still 48 hours behind the record.

Finally, picking up the wind, I'm frustrated that after the north Atlantic hurricane factory of 2005, we now have a very small swell and light winds. I need more wind and bigger seas so that we can push the boat harder and gain more miles. My prayers are answered as the winds hit 25kn and a 15ft swell runs with us.

Ed knocks on the cabin halfway through the night. The winds have increased, and the swell is bigger. They are understandably spooked; we haven't trained for these conditions. I jump on the oars with Birdy on the rear seat, controlling the rudder.

"Right, Birdy, you need to be on the ball with the rudder. We need to go straight down the waves when we catch them. If you lose it and we go right or left, we will probably capsize and be in a world of hurt."

We get a feel for the conditions. It's pretty big out here, and at night, the swell always looks bigger. I'm enjoying the challenge of being on the oars in a big sea. Sizeable waves come in, and we surf them beautifully, cranking the speed up to 11kn. As the end of our watch approaches, a 30ft wave comes through. We pick it up and scream down the face.

Hello, hello, I'm in a place called vertigo!

The tune is back. We lose control as we hit 16kn and career to port.

Shit.

Birdy manages to go hard to starboard just at the right time, and we recover. We are fighting all the way to try to make up time. I have an awesome team.

Three days out of Barbados, we have light headwinds that slow us. The realisation that we are unlikely to break the record sinks in. It's hard on the team, but everyone remains focused on crossing in a respectable time. It's a shame we haven't seen more wildlife, but a beautiful sailfish greets us 50 miles out from Barbados.

There's a strong onshore wind, and there's no way we can land on the east coast of the island, so I set a course to clear the island's northern tip to approach and land on the western side. I have to be very careful, as the approaches are a maze of dangerous reefs ready to tear the boat wide open. Horse Shoe Bay is the first land that greets us, and with the following swell, flying fish skim over the top of our boat. We row around the northern tip of the island before seeing a Coast Guard ship just north of Archer's Bay. On board is an old friend, Louay, who is coordinating the media. According to the rules of unsupported rows, a boat must not receive any assistance small or large at any stage of the voyage. Louay knows the rules, and the Coast Guard stands off.

The official clock for our recorded time stops when we touch land. Just south of Hangman's Bay, I'd identified a pier that appeared like a cement factory on the chart. I navigate oarsmen Tom and Birdy through the reef to the pier. Offering a very British celebration, I shake the team members' hands calmly and say a simple well done.

Despite an impressive rowing rate—making up 48 hours was unheard of—the four days of adverse winds cost us the Blue Ribbon of ocean rowing. We are exactly 48 hours behind the record set by the 11-man French team in 1992, but I know that every man on my team has done a sterling job. We still set a very respectable time of 37 days and 8 hours, making us the second-fastest four ever across the Atlantic. The team gelled, supported each other, and worked incredibly hard on the oars, and I'm honoured and very proud to be their captain.

The Coast Guard boat races towards us, and Louay shouts, "Domster! I've got good news and bad news. The good news is I've got you sponsored by Mount Gay Rum. The bad news is that I need you sober for interviews in Bridgetown."

It's great to see Louay. He'd been with me in St John's so understands what an important moment this is for the team and me.

The Coast Guard gives us a tow down to Bridgetown, where, on approach to the harbour, we row in to a very warm welcome. I light my handheld flare, which is a tradition for solo sailors, and as we row in the billowing red smoke, it takes me back to the north Atlantic as I signalled to Rescue Flight 133 that I was alive.

The cameras click on the dockside, this time recording a team that has crossed the Atlantic in one of the fastest rows in history. The smoked fills the deck. The guys are coughing and spluttering from the smoke, so they don't see the tears roll down my face… I'M ALIVE AND KICKING.

> "Twenty years from now you will be more disappointed by the things that you didn't do than by the ones you did do. So throw off the bowlines. Sail away from the safe harbor. Catch the trade winds in your sails. Explore. Dream. Discover."
>
> - Mark Twain

Epilogue

Pirates in the Mist

The Atlantic rowing campaign was to be my last official expedition, but I was nowhere finished with my adventures on the high seas.

Piracy had taken a turn for the worse. Since hitting dry land in Barbados, the Gulf of Aden had seen four ships hijacked, and the cruise liner the *Seabourn Spirit*, with 119 passengers, had been sprayed with automatic fire and accompanied by an RPG rocket attack for good measure. The crew had managed to repel the attack and continue on its voyage through the Indian Ocean. These were changing times; pirate tactics were getting bolder and their actions more violent.

Red Sea, December 2007

Four days out of the Suez Canal heading south, I'm busy preparing defences on board super yacht *Drumbeat*, which is a beautiful 170ft Ed Dubois twin-masted sailing ketch. I'm working for the first time with Marcel, a former member of the elite Israeli Mossad Intelligence Unit. He first served with Israeli Special Forces and was then recruited into Kidon, a Mossad assassination unit. During operations in Beirut in the 80s, his team had Yasser Arafat placed in their sights until a radio order by a top government official allowed him to live.

Marcel's heritage means that he holds a French passport, which is very handy for an Israeli travelling through the Middle East, especially in Egypt, where we boarded. In many cases, visas are refused to Israeli nationals who are trying to enter Egypt. Marcel is in his mid-50s and has put on a few pounds, but he is still very much on top of his game. We need to be: the security company that brought us together hadn't supplied us with weapons, and we could be up against pirates armed with AK47s and RPGs. While 15 years in the Royal Marines taught me to overcome the issues of operating without the right kit for the job, I always had the morbid comfort of a firearm.

We have to get creative. To increase our odds, we need to have the element of surprise and a plan. Spending four days on the Red Sea has given us time to prepare our entry into the Gulf of Aden, which would later become known to many navies as "Pirate Alley." We search the yacht to find things we can turn into weapons. We convert flares and the yacht's pyrotechnics into lethal booby traps to rig on likely pirate boarding points. The main part of the plan is, first, psychological: activating a series of loud blasts on the yacht horn, the pirates would know we'd seen them. The crew would muster to their emergency positions, and either one of us, disguised in a balaclava would overtly move out of sight to try to create an illusion that we're ready for the pirates, who would now be unsure of what or how many would be waiting for them. A super yacht owned by a rich guy may have Seal Team 6 on board, and this is exactly what we are trying to project. In reality, we are two unarmed guys, and we can only reveal our hand if they decide to hijack us—or worse. It's impossible to negotiate with these guys; a number of ships have already been hijacked and the crew members killed. We can't take that chance.

If pirates attempt to board, we have to use maximum violence to repel the attack. Our first line of defence is the host of pyrotechnics rigged on the stern. They would blast out hot white phosphorus and shrapnel to kill or maim as many pirates as possible. In the shock of the blast, we'd then lob Molotov cocktails into their skiff to burn them alive. We'd then fall back to our defensive positions, ready for the next attack if any surviving pirates wanted another go. Should any board successfully, using our knowledge of the yacht and working together, we'd use fire axes and knives to kill and disarm any pirates to then use their weapons. The tables would turn badly for them. A skinny, untrained Somali thug is no match for a former Royal Marines Commando and Mossad assassin armed with AK47s.

While the action unfolded, the crew would be safely in the engine room below the waterline and out of harm's way but would be in radio contact, so we order steering directions to make boarding as hard as possible. Marcel and I also discussed that should the situation arise, we'd leave the crew in the engine room while we clean up and throw any body parts or bodies over the side. Our job is to protect the crew, and seeing such horrific scenes could have an adverse effect, and while loose lips in the yacht club may show bravado, it could be bad for business.

"Captain, the most important part of this voyage is that we must pass through the straights of Bab el-Mandeb at night with all the lights off."

"Not a problem. I will adjust our course accordingly," assures the captain.

Captain Mark Stevens is around my age and is a very good sailor. He has a loyal, hard-working crew that makes our job a lot easier.

Marcel and I settle into our watch routine with the crew. We approach Bab el-Mandeb with no lights; we are a fully darkened ship. The straits are a narrow entry point that separates the Gulf of Aden from the Red Sea. The aim of going through at night is to enter the gulf without alerting pirates to our presence. From now on, night lights would be off for the remainder of the trip to the Maldives.

In the morning, the captain approaches Marcel and me. "Hi, guys. We have just received this piracy report over the Mini-C."

"ALL SHIPPING: PIRATE ACTIVITY REPORTED 30 MILES SOUTH of AL MUKALLA YEMEN. GENERAL CARGO VESSEL APPROACHED BY 21 SKIFFS UNDERWAY. SKIFFS ATTEMPTED TO BOARD FOR ONE HOUR. VESSEL AND CREW EVADED THE SKIFFS. ALL SHIPS EXERCISE EXTREME CAUTION AND REPORT ALL ACTIVITY TO IMB PIRACY REPORTING CENTRE."

We plot the attack position on the chart and decide that we have no option other than to sail straight down the middle of the gulf. There is danger on both the Yemen and Somalia coasts; we are caught between the devil and the deep blue sea. Marcel and I discuss this development. Twenty-one boats is a lot, but we have a plan to stand and fight, and I'm confident that Marcel is a good guy to back me up.

The wind has dropped since we've entered the gulf, and visibility is deteriorating as haze forms on the calm sea and the sea state is low. It's a perfect day for pirates. On the morning of day two, morning dew makes the haze even thicker. Steve the deckhand is busy with the daily ritual of wiping condensation from the decks; super yacht crew members spend most of their days with a chamois in their hands.

"Dom, skiff!" shouts Steve.

I jump up to the fly bridge. "Shit." It isn't just one looking on our portside; I count eight.

"Marcel, get up here!" I shout down the radio.

I count another six by the time Marcel and Captain Mark arrive.

"Sound the alarm, and get the crew down below." I look at Marcel the only way soldiers do—with resolve. "It's them."

Marcel jumps down to the stern to set up the ambush and prime our surprise. I observe through binoculars while slipping into my body armour. One skiff is 100m from us, the man at the stern trying frantically to start his outboard motor. He looks right at me, and two other skiffs that catch my attention are also trying to start their engines.

"Marcel, it looks like we've woken them up."

The pirates aren't ready. Their engines are cold from the condensation. This is a big break for us.

"Captain, give us everything you have on the engines and steer straight. No more evasive manoeuvres." We need speed.

The skiffs disappear into the haze, and the fumes from the Caterpillar engines cover the boat as we increase revs. I hear one outboard start. Then another. Then another.

"Shit." We're not out of the woods yet.

"I hear three. You?" Marcel says on the radio.

"Roger three," I confirm.

Three is not good, but it's a shitload better than 20. The skiffs are on the move. We hear their engines, but ascertaining which direction they are travelling in is proving difficult. We wait in silence. One skiff engine is getting louder and is approaching possibly 400m off our portside, but I can't see anything through the haze. They are hunting us.

"Captain, thirty degrees to starboard slowly." We need to put some distance between the skiff and us, but I don't want our wake to give us away in these flat, calm conditions. The noise from the other skiffs has faded away, but this skiff is close by.

"Dom, I think it's moving away; it sounds fainter."

"Roger that." I listen intently and then tell the captain to continue at his fastest course for around two hours to put some distance between the skiffs and us.

Marcel and I remain in our muster positions for another two hours, but it looks as if we are in the clear. Marcel and I look at each other and exchange knowing smiles. We've been really lucky. Without the haze, we could have been in a world of hurt.

This is the start of an incredible adventure fighting the pirates of Somalia. It will see me build the biggest private navy since the East India Company.

But that's another story...

Endnotes

[1] knot: a unit of speed equivalent to one nautical mile per hour

Printed in Great Britain
by Amazon